KT-219-969

PLANETS David A. Rothery
PLANTS Timothy Walker
PLATO Julia Annas
POLITICAL PHILOSOPHY David Miller
POLITICS Kenneth Minogue
POSTCOLONIALISM Robert Young
POSTMODERNISM Christopher Butler
POSTSTRUCTURALISM Catherine Belsey
PREHISTORY Chris Gosden
PRESOCRATIC PHILOSOPHY Catherine Osborne
PRIVACY Raymond Wacks
PROBABILITY John Haigh
PROGRESSIVISM Walter Nugent
PROTESTANTISM Mark A. Noll
PSYCHIATRY Tom Burns
PSYCHOLOGY Gillian Butler and Freda McManus
PURITANISM Francis J. Bremer
THE QUAKERS Pink Dandelion
QUANTUM THEORY John Polkinghorne
RACISM Ali Rattansi
RADIOACTIVITY Claudio Tuniz
RASTAFARI Ennis B. Edmonds
THE REAGAN REVOLUTION Gil Troy
REALITY Jan Westerhoff
THE REFORMATION Peter Marshall
RELATIVITY Russell Stannard
RELIGION IN AMERICA Timothy Beal
THE RENAISSANCE Jerry Brotton
RENAISSANCE ART Geraldine A. Johnson
REVOLUTIONS Jack A. Goldstone
RHETORIC Richard Toye
RISK Baruch Fischhoff and John Kadvany
RIVERS Nick Middleton
ROBOTICS Alan Winfield
ROMAN BRITAIN Peter Salway
THE ROMAN EMPIRE Christopher Kelly
THE ROMAN REPUBLIC David M. Gwynn
ROMANTICISM Michael Ferber
ROUSSEAU Robert Wokler
RUSSELL A. C. Grayling
RUSSIAN HISTORY Geoffrey Hosking

RUSSIAN LITERATURE Catriona Kelly
THE RUSSIAN REVOLUTION S. A. Smith
SCHIZOPHRENIA Chris Frith and Eve Johnstone
SCHOPENHAUER Christopher Janaway
SCIENCE AND RELIGION Thomas Dixon
SCIENCE FICTION David Seed
THE SCIENTIFIC REVOLUTION Lawrence M. Principe
SCOTLAND Rab Houston
SEXUALITY Véronique Mottier
SHAKESPEARE Germaine Greer
SIKHISM Eleanor Nesbitt
THE SILK ROAD James A. Millward
SLEEP Steven W. Lockley and Russell G. Foster
SOCIAL AND CULTURAL ANTHROPOLOGY John Monaghan and Peter Just
SOCIALISM Michael Newman
SOCIOLINGUISTICS John Edwards
SOCIOLOGY Steve Bruce
SOCRATES C. C. W. Taylor
THE SOVIET UNION Stephen Lovell
THE SPANISH CIVIL WAR Helen Graham
SPANISH LITERATURE Jo Labanyi
SPINOZA Roger Scruton
SPIRITUALITY Philip Sheldrake
STARS Andrew King
STATISTICS David J. Hand
STEM CELLS Jonathan Slack
STUART BRITAIN John Morrill
SUPERCONDUCTIVITY Stephen Blundell
SYMMETRY Ian Stewart
TEETH Peter S. Ungar
TERRORISM Charles Townshend
THEOLOGY David F. Ford
THOMAS AQUINAS Fergus Kerr
THOUGHT Tim Bayne
TIBETAN BUDDHISM Matthew T. Kapstein
TOCQUEVILLE Harvey C. Mansfield
TRAGEDY Adrian Poole
THE TROJAN WAR Eric H. Cline
TRUST Katherine Hawley
THE TUDORS John Guy

Geopolitics: A Very Short Introduction

VERY SHORT INTRODUCTIONS are for anyone wanting a stimulating and accessible way into a new subject. They are written by experts, and have been translated into more than 40 different languages.

The Series began in 1995, and now covers a wide variety of topics in every discipline. The VSI library now contains over 350 volumes—a Very Short Introduction to everything from Psychology and Philosophy of Science to American History and Relativity—and continues to grow in every subject area.

Very Short Introductions available now:

Available soon:

For more information visit our website
www.oup.com/vsi/

Klaus Dodds

GEOPOLITICS

A Very Short Introduction

OXFORD
UNIVERSITY PRESS

OXFORD
UNIVERSITY PRESS

Great Clarendon Street, Oxford, OX2 6DP,
United Kingdom

Oxford University Press is a department of the University of Oxford.
It furthers the University's objective of excellence in research, scholarship,
and education by publishing worldwide. Oxford is a registered trade mark of
Oxford University Press in the UK and in certain other countries

© Klaus Dodds 2014

First edition published 2007
Second edition published 2014

Impression: 2

Published in the United States of America by Oxford University Press
198 Madison Avenue, New York, NY 10016, United States of America

British Library Cataloguing in Publication Data
Data available
Library of Congress Control Number: 2014936756

ISBN 978-0-19-967678-1

Printed in Great Britain by
Ashford Colour Press Ltd, Gosport, Hampshire

*For Theo
(24 February 2006–22 May 2007)*

Acknowledgements

I owe a debt of gratitude to colleagues at Oxford University Press
who graciously consented to a second edition. My sincere thanks to
Andrea Keegan, Emma Ma, Edwin Pritchard, Deborah Protheroe,
Kate Farquhar-Thomson and Chloë Foster who support VSI
authors in the production process and then arrange opportunities
for them to speak at festivals and other public events. Appearing at
the Oxford Literary Festival remains a great privilege.

When I wrote the first edition, I deliberately tried to make it
contemporary in focus and after seven years or so some of the
references to say the War on Terror and the conflicts in
Afghanistan and Iraq appear to have been overtaken by a coterie
of events including the so-called 'Arab Spring', the global financial
crisis, mass surveillance revelations, and a host of other
circumstances around the world. While I am not 'banking'
(forgive the financial pun) on a third edition, it is a welcome
opportunity to introduce some conceptual updating as well as to
reflect on the difference that a wider variety of agents, objects,
sites, and performances make to the business of geopolitics.

I remain appreciative of my colleagues at Royal Holloway,
University of London. After 20 years, it remains a wonderfully
productive place to research and teach. I also thank my
undergraduate and graduate students for their passion for all

things pertaining to geopolitics and security. Peter Adey was kind enough to comment on some of the new material. Kay Clement helped proof read the book at the final stages.

The second edition of this book remains dedicated to my late son Theo for bringing us so much joy in his brief life. My family has played a vital role in my rehabilitation over the intervening period between the first and second editions, and for that I am truly thankful.

Contents

List of illustrations

Geopolitics

Chapter 1
It's essential to be geopolitical!

Geopolitics is a slippery term. While it might be thought of as referring to the varied geographies of international relations, it has often been used to infer a hardheaded approach to the world in general. A way of looking and behaving that concentrated on the interrelationship of territory, resources, and strategic access, without being seduced by idealized understandings of what should happen. Geopolitics for many of its users was about being realistic, even cynical, about states and the international system. When Robert Strausz-Hupe, the founder of the right-wing Foreign Policy Research Institute in the United States urged his readers in 1941 that 'It is smart to be geopolitical' he was perpetuating this particular intellectual conceit. The knowing citizen, in other words, was a geopolitical one comfortable with the idea that what made the world go around was the quest for territorial/resource advantage. Given that the timing of his message was in the midst of the Second World War, this appeal to be geopolitical was also about consolidating an internationalist perspective in the aftermath of America's entry into war with Japan and later Germany.

At times of war and crisis, it is perhaps not surprising that the focus on territorial and resource-related themes looms large. In recent years, our newspapers, television screens, and Internet news sites have been filled with stories about territorial-ethnic struggles in the Middle East, resource intrigue in the Arctic and Southern Ocean, land purchasing in Africa, food insecurity, and austerity programmes throughout the world. Anxieties continue to abound about resource shortages and population pressures, in a manner reminiscent of earlier fears about a 'population time bomb' in the early 1970s. Little wonder, perhaps, that 'geopolitics' is enjoying a renaissance. It all seems a far cry from the 1990s, when some were predicting the global spread of democracy, the triumph of market capitalism, and cultural globalization. Some even suggested that 'geopolitics' was likely to be redundant. The 11 September 2001 attacks and subsequent War on Terror shook some of that prevailing confidence, and economic crisis, from 2007–8 onwards, has merely consolidated a sense of a discombobulated world. But it is also important to bear in mind that many other places and peoples are implicated in 'geopolitics', some of which barely get reported or commented upon by the mainstream Anglophone media. One example might be the Central African Republic, which has been described as on the 'verge of genocide' as it remains in the grip of state and non-state violence involving Ugandan warlord, Joseph Kony.

I want to change that earlier *appeler aux armes* to 'it's essential to be geopolitical'. None of us has a monopoly on smartness, and while we might disagree on what is essential and what is not, I think there is great value in being able to think about the world in geopolitical terms. But in so doing, I also want to stress that geopolitics is as much about the high profile and dramatic (e.g. the Obama administration's policy to pursue high-profile terrorist targets in Pakistan and Yemen, see Figure 1) as it is about the everyday, the banal, and the apparently mundane (e.g. children reciting the pledge of allegiance in classrooms all over the United States). If geopolitics continues to appeal then it does so because it offers a promise. The promise of a 'view of the world' where the fundamentals are revealed and which is thus uncluttered with mundane and trivial detail. My aim in this book is, in large part, to

1. President Obama and colleagues, including Secretary of State
Hillary Clinton, watch for news of Osama Bin Laden's real time
capture (and eventual death) in Pakistan

say that the mundane and the trivial provide 'us' with some
fundamental insights into how 'our' world works.

Towards an understanding of geography and geopolitics

So what exactly is geopolitics? If you were to Google the term
'geopolitics' at any one time, you will see millions of hits. Anyone
brave or perhaps foolish enough to wade through even a fraction
of those potential references would not necessarily emerge any the
wiser with regards to an absolute definition of geopolitics. To
paraphrase the social theorist Michael Mann, geopolitics, like
most terms that have attracted academic attention, is slippery.
More often than not, it is used by politically conservative
journalists and pundits such as Thomas Barnett of the *Esquire*
magazine, Thomas Friedman of the *New York Times*, or the
former US Secretary of State Henry Kissinger as a shorthand
term, intended to convey a robust attitude towards political action

3

using taken-for-granted geographical templates such as the 'axis of evil' and 'outposts of tyranny'. Rather than take those terms for granted (or simply mock them), it is vital that we explore the sorts of consequences that follow from dividing the world into particular zones.

Let me start by addressing what is meant by the term 'geography' before moving on to geopolitics. Geography is a diverse academic and popular field and for many people, especially those who are not geography graduates, there is a tendency to focus either on the physical geographies of the earth (e.g. mountain ranges, maritime passages, rivers, and so on) or categories such as distance and territory. Some might also think readily of objects such as maps and charts when it comes to appraising the 'geographical'. Other commentators will tell you that geography is about charting how climates and environments have fundamentally determined human societies. It is still not uncommon, for example, to read that hills, rivers, coasts, seas, and mountains have shaped personal and collective identities, practices, and ideologies.

My point is to claim such things, even if they have any kind of intellectual merit, is to reduce geography to physical terrain with extraordinary powers to shape human practices. A crude kind of environmental determinism then prevails. Tribal peoples living in the Yemen, for example, resist attempts to govern their movements because their mountainous environments have made them that way. I am struck, over and over again, by how mountains in particular act as an explanatory factor in that regard. Mountains make people and as such we can explain, even predict, human history. Or so that particular story might go. At its worst, this kind of determinism can be mobilized by others outside those particular milieus to justify in the case of Yemen a series of policies designed to minimize direct contact with these 'tribal peoples'. The use of the drone, for example, appears to be an ideal accomplice to direct contact with these geographically unstable regions. What might get missed is how Yemeni society is as complex as many others regardless of geographical environments.

But geopolitics provides ways of looking at the world that often embrace a simplified view of geography. Maps, tables, and photographs can play their part in simplification. But so do seemingly innocent sounding terms like heartland, pivot, arc, and borderlands. Geopolitics offers for many a reliable (read objective) guide of the global landscape by using geographical descriptions, metaphors, and templates such as those listed above but also many others over the decades such as 'iron curtain', 'Third World', and/or 'rogue state'. Each of these terms is inherently geographical in the sense that places (rather than spaces) are identified and branded as such. It then helps to generate a simple model of the world, which can be used to advise and inform foreign and security policy making. This idea of geopolitics is by far the most important in terms of everyday usage in newspapers, radio, magazines, and television news, which also tends to reduce governments and countries to simple descriptors such as 'London', 'Washington', or 'Moscow'. Geopolitics works as an academic and popular practice by enrolling geography and the geographical. Labels like the 'iron curtain', the 'pivot', and the 'axis of evil' have a heuristic value. They help to inform and instruct audiences about the geographical certainties underlying world politics.

But there might be another way of seeing geopolitics and geography. My preferred starting point is to think of the geographical as something that is made and remade. Geography, as its etymology suggests, is a form of earthly writing, an activity that highlights the power of agents and organizations to write over space, to occupy space, to organize space, and to create places invested with particular visions and projects. Geography in this context is always in a state of becoming rather than something just 'fixed' like a mountain range—which turns out to be anything but 'fixed' as physical geographers and geologists understand only too well. I see the geographical as inherently strategic—subject to both human intervention and invention but also capable of being enabled, frustrated, emboldened, and disrupted by earthly forces and processes such as weather, dirt, ice, rivers, and ocean currents.

The aim here is to show how geopolitics gets used, and with what consequences, especially in everyday life. Many geopolitical writers take the global stage as their starting point and remain preoccupied with what we might call 'high politics' such as war, diplomacy, and statecraft. Armed with their 'god's eye view of the world' and accompanying maps, the world being described is one that is environmentally deterministic and state-centric. It is also likely to be one where certain actors and factors get over-determined—the rise of China, the decline of the United States, the Arab Spring, peak oil, and so on. While all of these things are important in their own terms, it can quickly become rather abstract, disembodied, and inattentive to the complex interrelationship between people, institutions, and places. China may be 'rising' but 'rising' to what and where? Is everyone in China 'rising' and from where given that in the past it was acknowledged as one of the world's most advanced civilizations? Is China simply a particular geographical unit located in East Asia or something that manifests itself as much through networks and objects like trading circuits and electronic goods rather than simple measures such as naval strength and foreign direct investment levels?

So accounting for how agents, things, and relationships are made to matter geopolitically is an imperative for this author. I don't assume that geographical factors simply determine. Instead I ask—how is the geographical made to matter? The notion of the geographical or geopolitical imagination might be helpful at this point, and owes much to the writings of the late Palestinian-American scholar Edward Said. In his many works including his much-cited book *Orientalism* (1978), Said articulated an interest in how places were and continue to be imagined and represented in art, literature, music, and later in Western foreign policy-making communities. As a committed advocate of a Palestinian state, he was deeply sensitive to how communities such as the Palestinians or the wider Arabic world were understood, often in unflattering terms, as unstable, threatening, and/or exotic. This meant, he suggested, that particular cultural and political understandings of place and communities could rally policy makers and public opinion in ways that might be antithetical to the project of achieving an autonomous Palestinian community. Writing for much of his life in the United States, Said was deeply concerned that the mainstream media in that country was unsympathetic to the plight of the Palestinians and more likely to regard them as harbourers of terrorists than part of a dispossessed people confined to refugee camps, second-rate status Israeli citizens in some cases or, like himself, part of a wider diaspora. If Palestinians are understood in unflattering terms then it becomes all the easier for others such as pro-Israeli supporters to marginalize attempts to draw attention to the continued occupation by Israel of the West Bank or the consequences of the Israeli-built security wall. This is not to say that the state of Israel does think it has reasons to have security-related projects; rather it is to ask how and where these projects support a geopolitical imagination (and accompanying security practices), which is very different from that of Palestinians.

Geographical representations help to inform understandings of the world and in that sense we are all geopolitical theorists. Our understandings and experiences of geopolitics are radically different. Feminist scholars have been active in highlighting how those understandings and experiences are gendered. So when a state, for example, declares a 'state of emergency' the consequences for men and women will vary. Women protestors in the midst of protests in Cairo in 2012 and 2013, for example, found that the police and security forces were carrying out gynaecological examinations in order to assess whether they were 'pure' women. The inference being that these dissenting women who did not share the geopolitical world-view of the Egyptian state and its elites were improper, misguided, and corrupted. Race

7

and ethnicity can be another powerful marker of difference, as can sexuality. For many black and Asian people, especially over the last decade or so, the fear of terrorism has meant that their bodies and behaviours become more closely scrutinized than their white counterparts. But even then this does not account for how heightened airport security technologies have impacted upon others with bodily differences such as those who might be deaf or dependent upon artificial limbs. Sexuality can also be a marker of suspicion as well. Gay and lesbian communities might point to the fact that it was striking how often geopolitical agents such as Saddam Hussein and Osama Bin Laden were imagined to be 'faggots' rather than heterosexual men—the inference being, perhaps, that it was easier to construct a more troubling geopolitical vision of threat and danger if adversaries are imagined not to be straight men. So geopolitics can be a highly moralized as well as securitized way of looking at the world.

Linking geopolitics to popular culture

For this author, geopolitics is neither something that simply occurs in and around the State Department nor something simply manifested on television chat shows, newspaper leaders, and radio phone-ins. It can and is all of these things. Geopolitics can be highly visible and yet barely noticed. Take a highly visible example to start with. The State of the Union address is delivered by the American President to a Joint Session of the House of Congress in January of each year. It is a high-profile opportunity for a president to convey his (and note I have not had to use the word 'her') geopolitical vision for the country and the wider world. As part of that *tour d'horizon*, the State of the Union address frequently utilizes a whole series of geopolitical codes in order to rank countries and regions in order of their geographical significance, ranging from major allies to those considered to be clear and present dangers. The speech is televised and subject to extensive analysis in newspapers, television shows, and magazines. Moreover, coming from the leader of the most powerful state in the world, presidential speeches also enjoy extensive contemplation from international media organizations. Some men matter more than others and what those men choose to focus on is significant. President Obama does not really want to focus on drone attacks in Pakistan and Yemen and what the radical journalist Jeremy Scahill calls 'the dirty wars'.

Speaking in January 2002, only a few months after the 11 September attacks on the United States, the President's State of the Union address was a momentous event as many citizens looked to their Commander-in-Chief to make sense of events. American citizens were still in a state of shock. How was the President going to both reassure the populace and reassert America's sense of self-importance? As the speech unfolded, Bush deployed the following explicit geopolitical evaluation:

> Our second goal is to prevent regimes that sponsor terror from threatening America or our friends and allies with weapons of mass destruction. Some of these regimes have been pretty quiet since September the 11th. But we know their true nature. North Korea is a regime arming with missiles and weapons of mass destruction, while starving its citizens.
>
> Iran aggressively pursues these weapons and exports terror, while an unelected few repress the Iranian people's hope for freedom.
>
> Iraq continues to flaunt its hostility toward America and to support terror. The Iraqi regime has plotted to develop anthrax, and nerve gas, and nuclear weapons for over a decade. This is a regime that has already used poison gas to murder thousands of its own citizens—leaving the bodies of mothers huddled over their dead children. This is a regime that agreed to international inspections—then kicked out the inspectors. This is a regime that has something to hide from the civilized world.
>
> ... I will not stand by, as peril draws closer and closer. The United States of America will not permit the world's most dangerous regimes to threaten us with the world's most destructive weapons.
>
> (Applause)

9

This section of the address caused much interest amongst media and political commentators not least because of the phrase 'axis of evil' to describe the trio of Iran, Iraq, and North Korea. When the President of the United States and Commander-in-Chief of the US Armed Forces describes three countries as part of an 'axis of evil', people all over the world tend to notice. Unsurprisingly, the governments of those three countries strongly criticized the speech and denounced the United States in public ripostes designed in the main to reassure domestic audiences. From the President's point of view, the phrase 'axis of evil' was not only intended to act as a proverbial 'shot across the bows' of states that the United States disapproved of but also provided a simple geographical template of the world. The 2002 State of the Union address mattered greatly because it helped to cement a geopolitical imagination which positioned the WMD-holding regime of Saddam Hussein in Iraq as being intimately connected to the 11 September 2001 attacks. Despite there being no clear evidence to link that regime to Islamic militancy and terror networks, many Americans were content to accept the geographical linkage and this in turn helped the administration to persuade their citizens that an invasion of Iraq, after the earlier military action in Afghanistan, was a vital next step in winning the Global War on Terror. Domestic audiences matter because they consume and indeed reproduce those geopolitical imaginations— reproducing them in everyday conversations within the home, the café, and other public spaces (see Box 1).

Box 1. Bringing the terror home: rebooting James Bond

In 2005, James Bond, played by Daniel Craig, reappeared in *Casino Royale* and ushered in a very different kind of 007. Craig's Bond was meaner and leaner as he confronted a world composed of transnational criminal and terrorist networks. In earlier incarnations, there was always the evil genius's secret lair to storm but no more. Post 9/11, the screenwriters have invented a rather different geopolitical world where the Quantum network appears to be everywhere, even infiltrating the British spy organization, MI6 (*Quantum of Solace*). London was no longer immune.

In *Skyfall* (see Figure 2), the terror comes to London as a disgruntled MI6 agent carries out an audacious assault against the MI6 building in central London. A disillusioned Bond is forced to return early from the disastrous mission in Turkey to stop further chaos enveloping London. For British viewers, the gestures to the 7 July 2005 terrorist attacks are clear, the geographical mapping of danger is harder. No longer safely confined to other places, and often highly stereotyped such as North Korea (*Die Another Day*), the secret agent has to save London itself. Computer and logistical networks such as London's subway convey a geopolitical world where being mobile is more important than being rooted.

2. James Bond in *Skyfall* (directed Sam Mendes, 2012). The first Bond film to feature London as the primary target of danger

Sometimes, however, there may be other kinds of geopolitics that get barely noticed. There might be two types here. The first type is banal geopolitics; in other words a geopolitics that is barely noticed despite the fact that it is part and parcel of everyday life. One example is flags. If you travel to the French-speaking province of Quebec in Canada, you can notice an interesting array of flags hanging from people's houses. If the flag of Quebec is hanging outside a door you can probably assume that the occupant is French-speaking Quebecois (possibly with an interest in seeing an independent Quebec in the future and concerned with the wider francophone world). If you see the flag of Canada hanging outside a door then it might be reasonable to assume that the residents are supportive of the federation of Canada. Flag choices become bound up with particular geopolitical subject-positions. As an occasional visitor to Quebec, I am always fascinated by the distribution of flags and I have exactly the same reaction when I travel to other places, some deeply divided and some deeply cosmopolitan (or both) like Belfast, Jerusalem, and New York.

The second kind of geopolitics is deeply hidden and only comes to be commented upon when popular culture and media play their part in exposing it to further public scrutiny. While the film *Enemy of the State* (1998) imagined it, former National Security Agency employee Edward Snowden dramatically exposed a world where some states such as the United States and United Kingdom spy, with the assistance and enrolment of internet service providers and communication corporations, on their own citizens and other people around the world. Snowden's departure from Hawaii, via Hong Kong and eventually Moscow, was headline news in 2013 and drew attention to a world where geopolitics and security were being shaped by the covert analysis of big data sources. Thanks to newspaper exposés, citizens discovered the existence of Microsoft PowerPoint slides explaining the scale and extent of something called PRISM. PRISM (created in 2007) is a massive data-mining program operated by the National Security Agency based in Fort Mead in the US state of Maryland. Snowden alleged that this activity was far more widespread than the US public might have even suspected and that communications companies were being ordered to turn over details of customer telephone and internet calls and search histories respectively.

The term *popular geopolitics* is used in this book to convey a sense of how geopolitical representations and practices enter into the public domain and help, at the same time, shape understandings of elite geopolitics, as represented by political leaders and corporations. What the Snowden revelations suggest is that where categories such as the popular and the elite begin and end is complex. When the Snowden story broke, political commentators made reference to films such as *Enemy of the State* to try and convey to audiences what might be at stake in terms of surveillance and the sites and spaces of this military–industrial–communications complex. So popular cultural artefacts helped constitute understandings of geopolitics and the leakage of PRISM created a series of diplomatic incidents as US allies such as Australia, Brazil, Israel, and the United Kingdom developed their own strategies and practices as a response. On the one hand they expressed alarm at the scale of the surveillance against their own citizens but on the other hand they were forced to fight off accusations that they were complicit in spying on their own citizens in the name of the War on Terror. Either way we can expect new policies being developed on the subject of mass surveillance. In the case of Brazil, however, the Brazilian government expressed deep concern that they had been covertly spied upon. In September 2014, as you might expect, a movie entitled *Classified: The Edward Snowden Story* will be released and will play its part in due course in informing and enriching popular geopolitics just as novels by George Orwell contributed to earlier cold war geopolitical culture. In 1954, for example, the CIA funded the making of Orwell's famous novel *Animal Farm* into a film in order to inform Western audiences about the dangers of totalitarianism, including surveillance.

Structure of this book

The second chapter investigates the intellectual history associated with geopolitics. Despite the fact that most people using the term in newspaper and television reports, and/or the internet have no appreciation of its history, the ideas associated with geopolitics have changed over time. Engagement with this intellectual field differs markedly in the United States compared to Latin America, Germany, and Japan. The alleged connections between German geopolitics and Nazism were absolutely pivotal in shaping subsequent engagements. For example, very few scholars in either the United States or for that matter in the Soviet Union used the term geopolitics for nearly 40 years following the defeat of Nazi Germany in 1945. Why? They feared that they would in turn be accused of harbouring Nazi sympathies and ambitions. But that did not stop others and high-profile individuals such as Henry Kissinger and journalist Robert Kaplan will make guest appearances in this chapter.

Chapter 3 engages with the idea of geopolitical architecture and how our understandings of a world composed of an international system based on territorial states, exclusive jurisdictions, and national boundaries is enduring but not all-encompassing. What might be important here is to understand the relationship between fixity and flow. How do architectures seek to impose fixity on flows? And do architectures encourage fixity to be more flow like? The financial crisis of 2008 onwards has revealed some of this geopolitical work as markets and money inhabit various worlds and provoked widespread protesting in London, New York, and other places. The 'Occupy' movement was in large part about trying to fix flows. Sometimes national governments try to fix and stop flows by investing ever more in border policing, hoping that they can slow down and impede movement. In 2013, the British government admitted that it had no real idea quite how large the flow of illegal immigrants was to the United Kingdom. Alternatively, governments can struggle to manage the mobility of others and this can and does have tragic consequences in places such as the Mediterranean and North Africa.

Chapter 4 considers the relationship between geopolitics and identity politics. Geopolitical projects frequently pivot on ideas and practices about selfhood and others. When President Reagan described the Soviet Union as the 'evil empire', it was fairly clear that the United States was being understood as a global force for good. As a former Hollywood actor, he would have appreciated the idea that the Soviet Union was part of 'the dark side' possessing a human geography that was barely understood. The Soviet leaders were the Darth Vaders of world politics. The role of the other (in this case the Soviet Union and its peoples) was a vitally important element in American self-understandings. It not only helped to identify a prevalent danger but also reinforced the self-identity of the United States. As the chapter suggests, however, the relationship between geopolitics and identity is more complex, depending on a range of local, regional, national, and trans-national imaginations and interactions.

The final two chapters consider various elements of what I have already termed popular geopolitics. Chapter 5 investigates the role and significance of objects. We examine the role of a number of objects including maps, toys, flags, and pipelines. All of the above have been infused with geopolitical significance and enrolled and at times resisted geopolitical projects such as state building, energy security, citizenship, surveillance, and territorial domination. As a child, for instance, some of my strongest memories are of playing with Palitoy's 'Action Man' and constructing ever more fanciful geopolitical scenarios involving enemies involving both German and Soviet-style forces. So how do we account for the role of toys and play in the making of the geopolitical citizen? And all of this, in my case, was occurring against the backdrop of the cold war. No computer games for me.

The final chapter expands upon our examination of maps with a wider consideration of films, magazines, television, the internet, and radio and the ways in which they contribute to the circulation of geopolitical images and representations of territory, resources, and identity. One area of particular interest is post-9/11 cinema and television, and the manner in which screen plays and scripts have embraced the politics of fear, hope, and anger. Do films such as *The Kingdom* (2007) and the television series *Homeland* offer us important insights into how geopolitics is imagined and practised? Was it really the case that special agent Jack Bauer in the long-running television series *24* was causing great alarm amongst sections of the US military because there was a worry that America's public image around the world was being greatly damaged by repeated portrayals of torture and extraordinary measures?

Advocating a critical geopolitics

This *Very Short Introduction* to geopolitics is one that is avowedly critical in nature and scope. It is not rooted in environmental determinism. It does not hold to the view that mountain ranges and oceans act as 'force fields' on human activities. Making sense of geopolitics does not mean that we should be uninterested in physical geographies but rather we should think about how the earthly forces afford, encourage, block, and even forbid human worlds. It is not preoccupied with whether China is rising, the United States is declining, and the rest of the world is simply getting by. It does not offer a blueprint for 21st century geopolitics per se. There are other writers and armchair strategists who can provide such geopolitical services.

My goal is somewhat different. It is to situate geopolitics within everyday contexts. It is to insist that geopolitics is embodied and experiential—so what I mean is that geopolitics is impactful—sometimes dramatically and sometimes delicately. It is one in which objects (e.g. flags) and non-human actors and forces (e.g. hurricanes and ice) are seen to be operating alongside human agents and agency (hence the chapter on objects). And above all, it is an approach designed to encourage the reader to be critical of geopolitical reasoning and practices, especially ones that seek to simplify the complex relations between people and places. In my lexicography, I prefer to talk about sites and spaces rather than 'geographical facts' and I would advocate an approach that does not fixate on territorially defined states, big powers, and particular agents like politicians. If we do we miss a great deal. We neglect the role of different human agents such as women and indigenous peoples and non-human agents such as objects and animals. We might well underestimate the multiplicity of geopolitical sites that are available to investigate, including the home and the everyday. Finally, we need to ensure that a critical geopolitics does not merely speak, in the light of the above, to the interests of the powerful wherever they may be located. It is essential to be geopolitical.

Chapter 2
An intellectual poison?

Introduction

> Geopolitics presents a distorted view of the historical,
> political and geographical relations of the world and its parts.
>
> (Isaiah Bowman, 1942)

> All words have histories and geographies and the term
> 'geopolitics' is no exception. Coined in 1899, by a Swedish
> political scientist named Rudolf Kjellen, the word
> 'geopolitics' had a twentieth century history that was intimately
> connected with the belligerent dramas of that century.
>
> (Gearóid Ó Tuathail, 2006)

In 1954, Richard Hartshorne lambasted geopolitics as an
intellectual poison. During the Second World War, he had worked
in the Office of Strategic Services (the forerunner of the Central
Intelligence Agency) and helped to generate geographical
intelligence for the US military. He, like other geographical
scholars before him such as Isaiah Bowman, found geopolitics to
be intellectually fraudulent, empirically distorted, ideologically
suspect, and tainted by association with Nazism (and other
variants of fascism including Italian and Japanese) and its
associated policies of genocide, racism, spatial expansionism, and
the domination of place. Given this damning indictment, it is
perhaps not altogether surprising to learn that many geographers

in the United States and elsewhere including the Soviet Union were unwilling to enter this intellectual terrain. Within 50 years of its formal inception (and there is a pre-history to the coinage of 'geopolitics' including 19th-century writers such as Friedrich List), therefore, it stood condemned by a cabal of geographers and more importantly by writers contributing to widely read American periodicals such as *Reader's Digest*, *Life*, and *Newsweek*. To claim, therefore, that geopolitics has had an eventful intellectual history would be something of an understatement.

How had geopolitics first attracted such opprobrium? In November 1939, *Life* magazine published an article on the German geographer Karl Haushofer and described him as the German 'guru of geopolitics'. The article contended that geopolitics, as a scientific practice, not only gave Nazism a sense of strategic rationality but also invested National Socialism with a form of pseudo-spirituality. Both aspects were significant in shaping public and academic attitudes towards this subject matter. On the one hand, geopolitics was condemned as a fraudulent activity not worthy of serious scholarly attention but, on the other hand, the critics bestowed upon it extraordinary powers to strategize and visualize global territory and resources. The use of the term 'guru' was not, therefore, entirely innocent precisely because it conveyed a sense of Nazism being endowed with a supernatural spirit and wicked sense of purpose. By the fall of 1941, the *Reader's Digest* alerted readers to the fact that at least 1,000 more scientists were intellectually armed and ready to bolster the geopolitical imagination of Hitler and the German *Volk* (people). Frederick Sondern, writing for mass audiences in the *Reader's Digest* as well as in *Current History*, described a shadowy Munich-based organization called the Institute for Geopolitics that was intent on informing Hitler's plans for world domination. According to the author, the atmosphere was febrile:

> The work of Major General Professor Dr Karl Haushofer and his
> Geopolitical Institute in Munich, with its 1000 scientists,

technicians and spies [is causing great alarm]…These men are
unknown to the public, even in the Reich. But their ideas, their
charts, maps, statistics, information and plans have dictated Hitler's
moves from the very beginning.

Such was the concern about this shadowy institute and the
extraordinary powers attributed to German geopolitics that
President Roosevelt commissioned a series of academic studies on
the subject. While those experts were less convinced about the
claim concerning 1,000 scientists and technicians in the service of
Hitler, they concurred that geopolitics was providing intellectual
muscle to the practices associated with German statecraft
including invasion and mass murder. What made the accusation
of complicity even more damning was that some of the leading
authors such as Haushofer were closely connected to the Nazi
regime. This crossover between the academy and the world of
government was crucial in adding further credibility to the charge
that geopolitics was ideologically bankrupt and morally suspect.

By the time the Second World War was over, geopolitics stood
widely condemned as being the handmaiden of Nazism and a
whole post-war generation of scholars and their textbooks on
political geography simply decided to omit geopolitics from their
discussions. When one American-based geographer, Ladis Kristof
(father of the *New York Times* columnist Nicholas Kristof), tried
to resurrect the term in the United States in the early 1960s, he
was castigated by his colleagues and damned for even mentioning
the term geopolitics in print.

The origins of the 'science' of geopolitics

In order to understand the alarm and outrage felt by American
critics during the 1940s and beyond, it is necessary to appreciate
fully the genesis of geopolitics as an intellectual term. Coined in
1899 by a Swedish professor of political science, Rudolf Kjellen, it
has often been taken to signify a hard-nosed or more realistic

left margin: Geopolitics

approach to international politics that lays particular emphasis on the role of territory and resources in shaping the condition of states. This 'science' of geopolitics posited 'laws' about international politics based on the 'facts' of global physical geography (the disposition of the continents and oceans, the division of states and empires into sea- and land-powers). Reacting against what he perceived to be an overly legalistic approach to states and their conflicts with one another, the introduction of scientific geopolitics in the academic and government-orientated worlds of the 1890s and 1900s was opportune. As a portmanteau adjective, geopolitics attracted interest because it hinted at novelty—it was intended to investigate the often unremarked upon geographical dimensions of states and their position within world politics. Kjellen later became a Conservative member of the Swedish Parliament and was well known for his trenchant views on Swedish nationalism and foreign policy designs.

The claim to novelty is a little misleading and it helps only in part to explain why geopolitics became an attractive term and vibrant intellectual concern throughout continental Europe. Was geopolitics a 20th century academic reformulation of more traditional forms of statecraft and state calculation, previously carried out in ministries of foreign affairs and ministries of war through the 18th and 19th centuries, rather than in university classrooms? But there were also other intellectual contexts in which the significance of geography in shaping international political relations was discussed. The German writer, Friedrich Rich, is a good example of such an engagement. In his *The National System of Political Economy* (first published in 1841) he gave advice to German statesmen about the importance of geographical factors (e.g. the accessibility of a country to sea and land routes, the potential for territorial expansion, and resource wealth). Sarah O'Hara and Mike Heffernan have shown how many of the ideas associated with this nascent geopolitics were foreshadowed by government documents and press speculation.

While geopolitics arose in response to specific late 19th century concerns, it perhaps reflected more an act of academic colonization (in an era of major university expansion in Britain and continental Europe) of an activity previously conducted outside the academy.

Three factors contributed to the establishment of geopolitics as a distinct subject. First, economic nationalism and trade protectionism was on the rise as imperial European states such as Britain and France agonized over the shifting and increasingly interconnected nature of the global economy. The rise of the United States as a trading power created further unease amongst these European powers. Second, imperial powers pursued an aggressive search for new territories in Africa and elsewhere in the mid to late 19th century. While imperial accumulation was on the rise, European powers confronted each other over ownership and access to those colonial territories. Britain and France were embroiled in tense encounters in North Africa, and Britain and Russia continued to jostle and parry in Central Asia under the sobriquet of the 'Great Game'. The famous British geopolitical writer Halford Mackinder described the new era as post-Columbian in the sense that the era of European exploration and colonization in the aftermath of Columbus's landing in the Americas in the 1490s was over. Ultimately, countries such as Britain and Germany engaged in rearmament, which provoked fears that conflict might materialize in Europe rather than simply erupt in faraway European-held colonies (see Box 2). Finally, the growth of universities and the establishment of geography as an academic discipline created new opportunities for scholars to teach and research the subject. The alleged scientific status of geopolitics was important in establishing claims to intellectual legitimacy and policy relevance.

The role of the United States in terms of economic and geopolitical influence further complicated these early geopolitical analyses of Europe and its imperial outposts. As contemporary

Box 2. Invasion novels and geopolitical anxieties

The invasion novel was a historical genre which gained considerable popularity between the 1870s and 1914. One of the most recognizable was George Chesney's *The Battle of Dorking*, a fictional account of an invasion of England by German armed forces. Others include Erskine Childer's *Riddle of the Sands*, which featured two British men on a sailing holiday who happen to prevent a planned German invasion when they chance upon a secret fleet of invasion barges. By 1914, over 400 books had been published about hypothetical invasions by overseas powers. Their popularity owes a great deal to the contemporary zeitgeist associated with Anglo-German rivalries, rearmament, and imperial competition in Africa and the Mediterranean. Public fears about 'foreigners' and German spy networks grew accordingly.

Invasion novels were also popular in Japan and emerged at a time when the Japanese confronted the Russians in 1904 for dominance of East Asia. In the United States, H. Irving Hancock wrote of an invasion by German forces and the occupation of the North-East Seaboard. American forces eventually repel the attackers.

observers such as Fredrick Jackson Turner opined, the American frontier was in the process of 'closing' as continental expansion came to its natural culmination. In the late 1890s, in the aftermath of the purchase of Alaska from Russia in the 1860s, the American Empire encapsulated the territories of Cuba, the Philippines, and Puerto Rico. Admiral Thomas Mahan, in his *The Influence of Sea Power upon History 1660–1783*, offered some sobering advice to the then Theodore Roosevelt administration. As a one-time president of the Naval War College, he was well placed to contribute to American strategic thinking. Looking back at Anglo-French naval rivalry in the 17th and 18th centuries, Mahan recommended that the acquisition of naval power was the single most important factor in determining a nation's geopolitical power. Sea power was the 'handmaiden of expansion' and an expansionist United States would need to be able not only to project its power across the vast Atlantic and Pacific Oceans but also to have the capacity to deter and/or defeat any rivals. The main threat, according to Mahan, lay with the German and Russian Empires and their maritime ambitions. His work was later to be translated and read with great enthusiasm in Germany and played a part in shaping German geopolitical thinking in the 1920s and 1930s, especially in the development of pan-regional theorizing.

The writings of Kjellen, initially attracted swift attention from German scholars, who explored in detail the relationship between politics and geography on a variety of geographical scales. In part, this movement of ideas owes much to geographical proximity and the interchange between German and Scandinavian scholars. German writers were, like Kjellen, deeply interested in conceptualizing the state according to its territorial and resource needs. Informed by variants of social Darwinism, the struggle of states and their human creators was emphasized, as was the need to secure the 'fittest' states and peoples. According to Fredrick Ratzel, Professor of Geography at the University of Leipzig, the state should be conceptualized as a super-organism, which existed in a world characterized by struggle and uncertainty. Trained in the natural sciences and conversant with the intellectual legacy associated with Charles Darwin and Jean Baptiste de Lamarck, Ratzel believed that the state was a geopolitical force rooted in and shaped by the natural environment. In order to prosper, let alone survive, in these testing circumstances, states needed to acquire territory and resources.

In his book, *The Sea as a Source of the Greatness of a People*, Ratzel identified both the land and sea as providing opportunities and physical pathways for territorial expansion and eventual consolidation. A strong and successful state would never be satisfied by existing limits and would seek to expand territorially and secure 'living space'. Rival states would also seek such spaces so, according to Ratzel, any state seeking to expand would be engaged in a ceaseless cycle of growth and decline. The search for living space was in effect a fundamental and unchangeable geopolitical law—quite literally a fact of life on earth. He was, unsurprisingly, a passionate advocate of a German empire and for a strong navy capable of protecting its overseas interests.

For many other writers as well, Germany's geographical location and historical experience at the centre of Europe was both a blessing and a curse—it had the potential to dominate the European continent but was also a victim of territorial loss and misfortune. Germany was, as Michael Korinman noted in 1990, 'a land of geographers', with some of the first established university faculties dedicated to teaching geography. On the eve of the First World War, German geographers such as Naumann and Partsch advocated a German alliance with the Austro-Hungarian Empire and a strong naval presence in order to expand its commercial objectives and territorial portfolio. With defeat in 1918 came the crushing realization that those ambitions were not likely to be achieved in the near future. The 1919 Peace Conference and the devastating financial and territorial settlement contained within the Treaty of Versailles sowed the seeds of resentment. When in the inter-war period the ideas of Ratzel were resurrected, geographers in France such as Paul Vidal de la Blache worried that these ideas concerning the state as a super-organism could be deployed to justify a resurgent Germany, determined to extract revenge for its earlier territorial and ethnic dismemberment.

Elsewhere in Europe, geographers and military officers were engaging with geopolitical ideas and relating them to a broader discussion on colonialism, national regeneration, and imperial mission. In Portugal, for instance, the emergence of Salazar's regime in the early 1930s precipitated public displays and engagements with Portugal's mission in regard to the wider

Portuguese-speaking world. In Italy, the new journal *Geopolitica* was created in order to facilitate further discussion over Italian geopolitical ambitions in the Mediterranean and Africa. In both countries, new maps were circulated in school textbooks and public murals with the purpose of instructing citizens about the geographical aspirations of these countries. In Spain, geopolitical discussion concentrated on Spanish colonial ambitions in North Africa and the government was anxious to project military power accordingly. Unlike Germany, Iberian geopolitical engagements were primarily preoccupied with colonial territories rather than reshaping the map of continental Europe.

When fears concerning a German military renaissance proved justifiable, the British geopolitical writer Mackinder advocated a Midland Ocean Alliance with the United States in order to counter any possible alliance between a resurgent Germany and the new Soviet Union. Although suggested in 1924, it is often understood to be one of the earliest proposals for a strategic alliance, which was later to be initiated by the North Atlantic Treaty Organization in April 1949. Although West Germany was an important cold war ally of the United States and Britain in the late 1940s, inter-war German geopolitical discourse was preoccupied with German territorial growth and cultural hegemony.

Geopolitics and Nazism

The most controversial element in the 20th century history of geopolitics comes with its alleged association with Nazism and Hitler's plans for global domination. The idea of a state being considered as a super-organism and moreover requiring 'living space' provided a dangerous if not wholly original backdrop to inter-war engagements with geopolitical ideas. For one thing, the notion of the state as an organism encouraged a view of the world that focused on how to preserve national self-interest in an ultra-competitive environment comprised of other rapacious states. Given the apparent stakes, the maintenance of the organism becomes critical and anything or anyone that threatens the healthy integrity of the state would need to be addressed with some vigour. Internally, therefore, those that control the state need to be vigilant. Externally, the health of the state is said to depend upon the relentless acquisition of territory and resources. Again this kind of thinking tends to promote a view of the world which inevitably cherishes a well-equipped military force ready and willing to act when the need arises (an idea that was to be taken up with great enthusiasm in other parts of the world particularly by post-1945 Latin American military regimes). It also promotes a moral detachment because these geopolitical writers are considered to be simply reporting back on certain geographical realities that are removed from social and political intervention (Box 3).

Box 3. Making sense of geopolitics

Geopolitics tries to give a scientific and reasoned explanation of the life of these super-beings who, with unrelenting activity on earth, are born, develop and die, a cycle during which they show all kinds of appetites and a powerful instinct for conservation. They are as sensible and rational beings as men.

(Late Chilean dictator and former Professor of Geopolitics, Augusto Pinochet, *Geopolitica*, 1968)

Critics have contended that Nazis such as Rudolf Hess and even Adolf Hitler deployed geopolitical insights and perspectives in order to promote and legitimate German expansionism in the 1930s and 1940s at the murderous expense of ethnic communities within Germany (the Jewish being the most obvious) and near neighbours such as Poland and Czechoslovakia. This association between geopolitics and Nazism remains much contested and relies in part on guilt by association. The notion of association is significant—it refers both to an intellectual connection but more significantly to a personal bond between some leading German geographers and highly placed Nazis.

At the heart of this accusation concerning the intellectual and political connections between geopolitics and Nazism lie the writings and social networks of Professor Karl Haushofer. Born in 1869, he entered the German army and finally retired in 1919 with the rank of major general. During his period of military service, he was sent to Japan in order to study their armed forces. Whilst on secondment (1908–10), Haushofer learnt Japanese and developed a keen interest in that country's culture. His interactions with Japanese military officers and geographers were critical in facilitating the emergence of Japanese geopolitical institutes such as the Japan Association for Geopolitics and the Geopolitics School at the University of Kyoto in the 1920s and 1930s. He was and remains a towering intellectual influence in the development of geopolitics not just in Germany and Japan but also in South America where his work was translated into Spanish and Portuguese and used extensively by the armed forces of countries such as Argentina, Brazil, and Chile.

After his retirement from the army, Haushofer became a professor of geography at the University of Munich and initiated the publication of the *Journal of Geopolitics* (*Zeitschrift für Geopolitik*) in the mid-1920s. As with his predecessor Ratzel, Haushofer believed that German survival would depend upon a clear-headed appreciation of the geographical realities of world politics. If the state was to prosper rather than just survive, the acquisition of 'living space', particularly in the East, was vital and moreover achievable with the help of potential allies such as Italy and Japan. An accommodation with the Soviet Union was also, in the short to medium term, wise because it would enable both countries to consolidate their respective positions on the Euro-Asian landmass. In order for Germany to prosper, its leadership would need, he believed, to consider carefully five essential elements, which lay at the heart of a state's design for world power: physical location, resources, territory, morphology, and population. If Germany were to be a 'space-hopping' state rather than 'space-bound', it would need to understand and act upon its territorial and resource potential.

Haushofer also promoted the idea of a theory of pan-regions, which posited that Germany and other powerful states such as Japan should develop their own economic and geographical hinterlands free from interference with one another. In order for Germany to dominate part of the Euro-Asian landmass, an accommodation with the Soviet Union was essential, as was a modus operandi with Britain, which was understood to be in control of Africa. Haushofer's prime geographical orientation was towards the East and he was an enthusiastic supporter of plans to develop a Berlin–Baghdad railway, which would enable Germany to project its influence in the Middle East and Central Asia. If developed, the railway would have facilitated access to oil supplies and (the British feared) a platform to disrupt trade to and from Asia. While the 1919 Peace Conference terminated German ambitions to pursue such a scheme, Haushofer's idea of pan-regions appealed to both traditional eastward-looking nationalists and industrialists eager to exploit the raw materials held in German colonies outside Europe.

While his ideas have been seen as intellectually underpinning Hitler's project of spatial expansionism and genocidal violence, critics contended (especially American observers in the 1940s) that these ideas mattered because of Haushofer's friendship with Rudolf Hess and his high-level involvement in German–Japanese negotiations in the 1930s and 1940s. Before his appointment as Hitler's private secretary and later deputy in the Nazi party, Hess was a student of Haushofer at the University of Munich. In his work *Mein Kampf*, Hitler evokes terms such as living space (*Lebensraum*) to expound upon his belief that Germany needed to reverse the 1919 Treaty of Versailles and seek a new geographical destiny involving Central and Eastern Europe.

There is, however, a critical difference between the two men. Unlike Haushofer who was largely preoccupied with spatial relationships and the organic state, Hitler placed a far greater emphasis on the role of people (in his case the Aryan race) in determining the course of history and geography. In other words, Hitler's obsession with race and his hatred of German and European Jewry did not find any intellectual inspiration from the writings of Haushofer. If the two agreed on anything, it was that the German state was a super-organism that needed 'living space' and associated territorial outlets. Despite his connections with Nazi officials, Haushofer's influence was on the wane by the late 1930s and early 1940s. He neither believed, as many Nazis did, that an international cabal of Jews and Communists was plotting to take over the world nor endorsed Hitler's obsession with the undue influence of German Jewry on the national welfare of Germany itself.

By 1941–2, German émigré intellectuals such as Hans Weigert, Andreas Dorpalen, Andrew Gyorgy, and Robert Strausz-Hupe had firmly implanted in the American imagination that German *Geopolitik* was Nazism's scientific partner in crime. Just as Haushofer was accused of being the evil genius behind the Nazi menace, his position and influence was, as we have noted, actually in decline. Furthermore, he thought that the German invasion of the Soviet Union in 1941 was strategically misguided and his close relationship with Rudolf Hess became a liability when it was discovered that Hess had secretly flown to Scotland in the same year in an attempt to seek peace with Britain. While the origins of Hess's mission are still unclear, it marked a turning point in the alleged influence of German geopolitical thinking on Hitler and his associates.

Haushofer committed suicide in 1946 after learning that his son Albrecht had been executed in April 1945 for his part in the bomb plot to kill Hitler in July 1944. One person who discussed geopolitical ideas with Karl Haushofer was the American colonel and Jesuit priest, Father Edmund Walsh. Interested in German and Soviet geopolitical writings, Walsh determined that Haushofer should not be indicted for war crimes even if he, like those aforementioned German émigré writers, was convinced that Haushofer was the 'brains-trust' of Hitler. As he noted in his 1948 book *Total Power*,

> the interrelation of cause and effect could no longer be disguised, as one invasion after another followed the broad pattern so long and so openly expounded in the writings and teachings of the master geopolitician.

Given Walsh's detailed interrogation of Haushofer in 1945, his academic judgement carried some considerable weight but even he stopped short of blaming Haushofer's intellectual corpus and personal relationships for Hitler's racist and expansionist policies.

Post-war decline in the United States

Having earned damnation and opprobrium from distinguished observers such as Edmund Walsh, who became the Dean of the United States Foreign Service at Georgetown University, it is not surprising that the reputation of geopolitics was in tatters. A new generation of American political geographers spurned the term and instead concentrated on developing political geography, which was carefully distinguished as intellectually objective and less deterministic with regard to the influence of environmental factors on the behaviour of states. In his important review of post-war Anglophone geopolitics, Leslie Hepple contends that the term 'geopolitics' dropped out of circulation of American political and popular life between 1945 and 1970. With very few exceptions, such as the Czech-born Professor of Sociology at the University of Bridgeport, Joseph Roucek, who published prolifically in academic and popular journals on topics such as the geopolitics of the United States or Antarctica, the term was studiously avoided. What is striking about all Roucek's articles containing the title 'geopolitics' is that he shows little to no interest in exploring the conceptual terrain occupied by the subject. For him, geopolitics is a useful shorthand (and apparently self-evident) term to highlight the significance of territory and resources.

Despite Roucek's spirited adoption, very few others were willing to employ a term so apparently tainted by an association with Nazism. The post-1945 period witnessed, if anything, the growing significance of the discipline of International Relations (IR) and realist theories, which addressed the role of the state in the international system. One notable moment in that disciplinary consolidation was in May 1954 when the Rockefeller Foundation convened a Conference on International Politics, designed to reconsider the 'state of theory in international politics'. This did not mean, however, that geographers and social scientists abandoned their interest in the geographies of the global political map. Geographers such as Nicholas Spykman (1893–1943) and later Saul Cohen recognized that the onset of the cold war meant it was more important than ever before to understand the territorial and ideological nature of the struggle between the Soviet Union and the United States. In his pioneering work, *Geography and Politics in a Divided World*, Cohen followed up an interest in Spykman's understanding of a patently fractured world.

If Spykman drew attention to what he called the rimlands of Eastern Europe, the Middle East, and South and South-East Europe, Cohen's later work focused on so-called shatterbelts and attempted to explain where the superpowers were likely to be locked into conflicts over territory, resources, and access. The geographical regions closest to the Soviet Union and later China were seen as the main battlegrounds of the cold war. Conflict and tension in Berlin, South-East Europe, the Middle East, Korea, and Vietnam seemed to add credence to that geographical view even if the high-profile Cuban missile crisis of 1962 demonstrated that the United States was extremely sensitive about the geographically proximate Caribbean basin.

Ironically, just as the term geopolitics was losing its credibility in the United States, Japan, Britain, and other parts of Europe, an argument emerged that American cold war strategy was implicitly inspired by geopolitical ideas. The National Security Council's NSC-68 document, delivered to President Truman in April 1950, warned of the Soviet Union's plans for world domination and possible geographical strategies for achieving that fundamental aim. Although dismissive of the Third World and its geographical diversity, NSC-68 was later to be supplemented by the so-called domino theory that warned that the Third World was vulnerable to Soviet-backed expansionism. Within a decade of the formation of the North Atlantic Treaty Organization in 1949, the United States created security pacts in Australasia (1951), Central Asia (1955), and entered into bilateral security arrangements with Japan and South Korea.

The few American political geographers such as Cohen who did comment explicitly on the cold war and US strategy were in agreement with general aims such as the containment of the Soviet Union but anxious to highlight the tremendous diversity of the Third World. In the eagerness to understand the global ambitions of the Soviet Union, Cohen warned American readers that they should not underestimate the profound geographical, cultural, and political differences between the Middle East, on the one hand, and South Asia, on the other. American strategists, such as George Kennan who worked at the Department of State during the Truman administration were, it was alleged, neglectful of those regional differences and NSC-68 was seen as geographically simplistic and overly concerned with representing the Soviet Union as a relentlessly expansionist threat from the East.

Geopolitical revival in the United States

Former Secretary of State Henry Kissinger is often credited with the revival of American interest in geopolitics even if his usage was far more informal than that of the turn-of-the-century exponents.

3. Henry Kissinger, former Secretary of State and National Security Advisor

Kissinger, as a German émigré and intellectual whose doctoral thesis had analysed 19th-century European geopolitical history, was not typical of secretaries of states in the post-1945 period (Figure 3). He was an intellectual heavyweight in the Nixon administration and a keen observer of the changing geopolitical condition of the cold war. The context of the time was critical—the cold war was entering a new phase of relative détente, even if the Soviet Union, the United States, and China were still suspicious of one another's motives and geopolitical ambitions. The United States was immersed in an increasingly unpopular conflict in Vietnam and Kissinger's use of the term geopolitics was in part an attempt to come to grips with a new strategic landscape. In the main, as Leslie Hepple has recorded, he uses the term to highlight the importance of global equilibrium and permanent national interests in a world characterized by a balance of power. Eager to promote a new relationship with China, he argued that Moscow's 'geopolitical ambitions' needed to be contained:

> Equilibrium was the name of the game. We did not seek to join China in a provocative confrontation with the Soviet Union. But we agreed on the necessity to curb Moscow's geopolitical ambitions. Peking's challenge was polemical and philosophical; it opposed not only Moscow's geopolitical aspirations but also its ideological pre-eminence. We agreed on the necessity of thwarting the geopolitical ambitions, but we had reason to become involved in the ideological dispute.

While the United States strived to contain the Soviet Union, Kissinger believed that existing American foreign policy had been too eager to promote a military response to this dilemma. Instead what was required was, in an era of relative American military decline, an approach that was flexible and attentive to new political possibilities such as developing relations with other powers like China (see Box 4).

Box 4. Subaltern geopolitics

Political geographers such as Jo Sharp and James Tyner argue that intellectual histories of geopolitics overemphasize Europe and the Americas at the expense of other engagements. In her research on East Africa, Sharp explores the writings of the former Tanzanian leader Julius Nyerere and his pan-African geopolitical imagination, which sought a 'middle way' between the binary geopolitics of the Cold War. Moreover, these post-colonial interventions have been increasingly recognized as an explicit challenge to geopolitical theorizing, which privileges the understandings and experiences of European and North American states, cultures, and world system.

In essence, subaltern geopolitics is not only predicated on exposing the Eurocentric nature of mainstream geopolitical theorizing but is also engaged in producing its own accounts of global politics, recognizing a shared vulnerability, collective interests, and past histories and geographies of inequality. Subaltern in this context never means marginal or small, rather it implies a critical stance towards those who would claim that their experiences and understandings should be considered universal.

Although Kissinger's usage of the term geopolitics has been described as fuzzy and vague, it nonetheless according to some scholars repopularized the term within American political culture and led to renewed formal academic reflection on global strategy. In terms of popularity, geopolitics was reintroduced into discussions on cold war politics alongside a host of other subjects that sought to connect global and regional issues. While few authors possessed a detailed appreciation of the term's tortured intellectual history, it served as an apparently useful moniker to highlight the significance of geographical factors in shaping political and military developments. Other leading political figures such as President Carter's Polish-born National Security Adviser, Zbigniew Brzezinski, were keen advocates of geopolitics and used the term to signal their interest in projecting America's strategic interests in an era of mounting global tension and, for those who were later to be called neo-conservative intellectuals, cited remorseless Soviet expansionism. The decision to fund and support resistance to the Soviet occupation of Afghanistan from 1979 onwards was informed by a geopolitical belief that further expansion had to be contained even if it meant that the United States and its regional allies such as Pakistan supported proxies in order to resist Soviet forces. As many have noted, this decision had important ramifications in terms of inspiring the creation of the Al-Qaeda terror network and producing battle-hardened veterans such as Osama bin Laden.

One of the most significant offshoots of this revival of geopolitics was the creation of the Committee on the Present Danger, which used geopolitics and other academic pursuits such as Sovietology (the study of Soviet government and society, sometimes described as 'Kremlin Watching') to contend that America had to be prepared to ditch policies of détente and balance of power in favour of a more aggressive approach which recognized that the Soviet Union was determined to extend its domination over the entire Euro-Asian landmass. Disappointed with the more dovish Carter administration, these intellectuals and academic commentators such as Colin Gray promoted a geopolitical world-view, which was later to be adopted by the Reagan administration. American foreign policy arguably pursued Soviet-backed proxies in Central America and Africa and more forcefully supported anti-Soviet regimes throughout the Third World. If that meant, for instance, supporting Saddam Hussein's regime in Iraq and countless military regimes in Latin America then so be it. Short to medium range nuclear missiles were stationed in Britain and West Germany as part of NATO's attempt to dispel any Soviet attempts to expand their influence into Western and Central Europe.

By the mid-1980s, geopolitical discussions within the United States were primarily shaped by a group of scholars strongly influenced by political realism and a desire to maintain American power in the midst of the so-called second cold war following the collapse of détente. Geopolitics once more became a shorthand term for great power rivalries and signalled the importance of the United States' pursuit of its own national interests in an anarchical world. United States foreign policy under Reagan was certainly more aggressive than under the Carter presidency and many intellectuals and policy makers associated with that administration were later to become members of the George H. W. Bush and George W. Bush administrations. Defense Secretary Donald Rumsfeld infamously shook hands with Saddam Hussein in the early 1980s yet was later instrumental in planning and executing the invasion of Iraq in 2003 and Hussein's overthrow and subsequent execution in December 2006.

Towards a critical geopolitics

About the same time that certain policy intellectuals were revisiting the term geopolitics in the context of the cold war, other writers were exploring a rather different conception of geopolitics. Later to be dubbed critical geopolitics, this approach was not realist in tone and outlook. As an approach to the study of international relations, realism has been highly significant, especially in the United States. It tends to assume that states inhabit a world which is anarchical because of an absence of a world government capable of restricting their actions. In the most basic forms of realism, self-interest and power projection are assumed as a consequence to be axiomatic. For many geopolitical writers, even if they do not refer to some of the high priests of realism such as E. H. Carr and Kenneth Waltz, they implicitly work with a model that is similar in outlook to many realists. For the Latin American generals preoccupied with their national security state in the 1960s and 1970s, the realist world-view coincided well with a geopolitical imagination filled with dangers and threats from communist forces inside and outside the state.

For the critics of this kind of realist inspired geopolitics, this jaundiced view of global politics is one-dimensional in the sense that it tends to overemphasize conflict and competition at the expense of cooperation and détente. The inter-state system has demonstrated a capacity, perhaps surprising to some observers, to collaborate and develop joint institutions, international law, and intergovernmental bodies such as the European Union and the United Nations. Moreover, a new generation of writers, inspired by different philosophical traditions, is sceptical of the claims of realist-inspired writers to simply 'tell it as it is'. In other words, far from presenting a disinterested world-view of global politics, it is

4. Robert Kaplan, journalist and author of *The Revenge of Geography*

profoundly shaped by particular representational schemas, which in turn reflect linguistic and cultural conventions. It is perhaps unsurprising that realist inspired geopolitics has found a warm reception in the United States, where it is common for writers to present their grand designs for the world as if they were disinterested observers simply telling their audiences a series of 'home truths' (Figure 4).

Feminist scholars such as Donna Haraway have been particularly significant in drawing attention to three things that follow from such intellectual conceits. First, we need to explore how geopolitics is made and represented to particular audiences. If we want to understand global politics we have to understand that it is imbued with social and cultural meaning. The current global political system is not natural and inevitable and the stories we tell about international politics are just that—stories. Some narratives are clearly more important than others and some individuals, such as the President of the United States and the President of Russia, are particularly vociferous and emphatic in determining how the world is interpreted. Hence world interest in the State of the Union address is considerable, just as it would be for a comparable discourse produced by other powerful states such as China and Russia. Would we be so interested in something similar produced by a political leader in West Africa or Central America? A current exception is the President of the oil-producing state Venezuela. Hugo Chavez's highly publicized criticisms of the Bush administrations and declarations that the President of the United States is a 'devil' are memorable as much for their undiplomatic tone as their capacity to exert influence over a world in the grip of high prices for oil and rising demand from the United States, China, and Europe. More generally, US–Latin American relations are being shifted as additional centre-left governments get elected in South America and a new, according to Chavez, 'axis of good' comes into existence.

Second, as a corollary of the above, geopolitics is conceived as a form of discourse, able to produce and circulate spatial representations of global politics. The focus here was on how policy-related language derived certain understandings of the current geopolitical situation and in turn contributed to an identity politics, which was critical in securing the United States' sense of itself. In an era that was largely defined as a battle of both ideas and influence, the cold war lent itself to this kind of geographical focus—attention was given as much to certain imagined geographies as it was to the actual manifestations of the conflict in places such as Afghanistan and/or Central America. Those imagined geographies included frequent representations of the United States, under the Reagan administration, as the 'leader of the free world' and the Soviet Union as the evil empire hell-bent on imperilling Western civilization.

Third, global geopolitics is entangled with questions of gender and other factors such as race and class. The everyday experiences of women and children and the strategies that they have to adopt in order to cope with geopolitical and geo-economic processes and structures need to be recognized as fundamentally different to the experiences of many men irrespective of their geographical location. Concepts such as territory, borders, and scale take on a different meaning when considering war rape in Democratic Republic of the Congo compared to the immigration of young men from North Africa to Southern Europe. If the global political boundaries are more porous to capital than to people, they are also more porous in general to men as opposed to women. As Cynthia Enloe has concluded, global geopolitics needs to be linked to the everyday geographies of gender relations in order to better understand the differential impact of national boundaries, security, conflict, and migration.

In order to understand better how geopolitics works, critical geopolitical writers have proposed a threefold division—formal, practical, and popular (Figure 5). The formal is concerned with the subject matter of this chapter. How do academics and commentators self-consciously invoke an intellectual tradition associated with geopolitics? Practical geopolitics refers to the policy-orientated geographical templates used by political leaders such as President Bush as they represent global politics. Finally, popular geopolitics includes the role of the media and other forms of popular culture, which citizens use to make sense of events in their own locale, country, region, and the wider world. All three forms are interconnected as academic writers and journalists routinely share ideas and discourses with one another and both groups have regular contacts with government officials and organizations. They are also immersed in the media and popular culture. Geopolitical frameworks can help both individuals and groups make sense of the world for themselves and a wider public. Phrases such as 'axis of evil' attract attention precisely because they are designed to simplify world politics and locate friends and

41

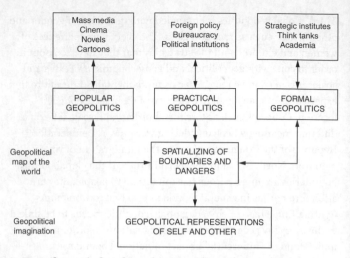

5. Formal, practical, and popular geopolitics

enemies. Presidents and prime ministers might use them initially (sometimes injudiciously) but these kinds of grand spatial abstractions provoke and promote discussions amongst journalists, pundits, and reading and listening public audiences.

The political geographer, Gearóid Ó Tuathail, has argued that this tripartite schema resides within a geopolitical culture, which shapes a state's encounter with the world. Britain's physical location on the edge of Europe, while it should not be seen as predetermining particular policy outcomes such as a commitment to the European integrative process, clearly has been significant in shaping cultural interpretations of geographical location. Also significant have been wartime experiences when Britain was forced to defend its national territories from German forces, including bombing raids and rocket attacks associated with the Blitz. Hence the shock and humiliation felt by some politicians such as Prime Minister Margaret Thatcher when the news broke that the Falkland Islands had been invaded by Argentina in April 1982. Political leaders and journalists rapidly invoked parallels with the

Second World War in an attempt to explain the dispatch of a naval taskforce, which ultimately prevailed against the Argentine forces in June 1982. During the conflict itself, Thatcher ensured that Britain had the support of the United States and this 'special relationship' was critical in ensuring access to weaponry and satellite information about Argentine military deployments. As with Prime Minister Blair over Iraq, Thatcher placed considerable importance on the Anglo–American relationship at the expense of a geopolitical tradition based on European Britain (see Box 5).

Box 5. Britain's four geopolitical traditions

1. Little England/Britain.
2. Cosmopolitan Britain.
3. European Britain.
4. American Britain.

(Adapted from Timothy Garton Ash, *Free World*, 2004)

Likewise, if we wished to understand better Russian geopolitical culture, we would need to appreciate, as the geographer Graham Smith noted, how political leaders and journalists have invoked three separate geopolitical traditions. First, the notion that Russia is a part of Europe and that the country needs to embrace Western models of social and economic development. Second, Russia is a distinctive Euro-Asian territory, with its own particular form of state and society. Finally, Russia, like Britain, is a 'bridge', in this case between Europe and Asia. At certain times, a particular geopolitical tradition might be dominant over others, such as President George W. Bush's apparent determination to pursue a geopolitical vision of a global United States, which is concerned with American hegemony and ability to project power in order to secure the national interest; and President Vladimir Putin's enthusiasm for Russia being an 'energy superpower' and distinct presence on the global stage independent of European and Asian neighbours.

This kind of appreciation of geopolitics as a broader cultural enterprise is not without precedent. Throughout the intellectual history of geopolitics, there are examples of individuals and groups committed to different forms of cultural and historical analysis, such as those found in critical geopolitics today. The work of Yves Lacoste and his Parisian colleagues deserves some mention because Lacoste was one of the first to really consider how geopolitics was a form of political and strategic knowledge. He penned a book in 1976, with the arresting English-language title of *Geography is Above All, Concerned with the Making of War*, which followed an earlier interest in the way American military planners used geographical knowledge of North Vietnam to target rivers and jungles in order to inflict ecocide (i.e. the deliberate destruction of local ecosystems in order to weaken adversaries) on the local population. He also examined the geopolitical theories of President Pinochet of Chile who was a former professor of geopolitics at the Chilean War College in the 1960s. The latter even penned a tome on geopolitics in which he advocated the view of the state as a super-organism and arguably put theory into practice when he helped to remove the socialist government of Salvador Allende on 11 September 1973. American support was judged to be critical and Henry Kissinger, then secretary of state, once noted with reference to Chile that

[I] don't see why we need to stand by and watch a country go communist due to the irresponsibility of its people. The issues are much too important for the Chilean voters to be left to decide for themselves.

Lacoste argued that geopolitical writers needed to be more self-critical and play their part in unmasking how geopolitics was implicated with expressions of militarism and state power. His journal *Herodote* continues to be the largest circulating geography journal in the French-speaking world and publishes critical analyses of contemporary events such as the Global War on Terror. Although Lacoste once noted that it was 'not in good taste to make reference to geopolitics', he has advocated an approach to the subject which is informed by critical regional analysis (i.e. demonstrating an appreciation for local and regional differences) and an understanding of the connections between geographical knowledge and political practice.

If geopolitics is worthy of further critical reflection, it is precisely because it has attracted a great deal of academic and popular attention, often with little appreciation of its controversial intellectual history. Presidents, prime ministers, and pundits love the term. It purports to deal with dangers, threats, space, and power. It helps to explain the world in simple terms—geographical templates such as the Third World often appear to have a reassuring solidity. It also empowers users to make predictions about the future direction of global politics. Journalists and academic commentators frequently invoke geopolitics when they wish to promote the next major development, whether it is the clash of civilizations, the rise of China, the End of History (and Geography), the new American Century, or the notion that Americans and Europeans are destined to misunderstand one another because they occupy different geopolitical universes.

Conclusions

The final part of our brief overview of geopolitics as an intellectual term has turned again to the United States and the English-speaking world. As I have indicated in earlier sections, this account needs to be complemented with a word of caution. The story presented here might be characterized as one of emergence, notoriety, decline, and revival. However, if this chapter had concentrated on the experiences of South America, a very different story would have emerged. For one thing, we would not have had to concern ourselves to the same degree with the alleged stigma of Nazism. In places such as the military academies of Argentina, Brazil, Chile, and Paraguay, which enjoyed a close relationship with the Italian and German militaries, military officers continued to teach and publish in the field of geopolitics throughout the post-1945 period. German geopolitical writings were translated into Spanish and Portuguese at a time when American geographers were urging their peers to avoid the term and its abhorrent connotations. In a continent dominated by military regimes for much of the cold war period, geopolitics flourished without much formal concern about connections to Nazism and associated policies of spatial expansionism and the domination of place.

Scholars in the Soviet Union who still considered geopolitics to be ideologically tainted with Nazism did not welcome this revival of interest, especially in the 1980s. While there is far more formal engagement with the term in post-Soviet Russia, memories of the Second World War and associated heavy Soviet losses of life played a part in shaping academic reactions to this new engagement of interest in North America and Western Europe. Fifty years later, this stigma appears to have been lifted and a new generation of mainly right-wing Russian and Uzbek commentators have used earlier geopolitical writers such as Halford Mackinder in particular to consider their countries' geopolitical destinies. One area of mounting interest is the strategic significance of Central Asia and the emergence of a so-called 'Great Game' between the United States, China, and Russia. The United States and China seek, much to the alarm of Russia, to extend their military and resource investments in a region characterized by largely untapped oil and natural gas resources in the Caspian Sea.

The final point to reiterate, apart from geopolitics' varied intellectual history, is that the last section on critical geopolitics should not be misunderstood. Only a small group of scholars in the United States and elsewhere would describe themselves as critical geopolitical scholars. In most countries, including the United States, most people using the term geopolitics have little interest in understanding that contorted intellectual history.

Moreover, they use geopolitics as a shorthand term usually intended to invest their work with a kind of rugged respectability and willingness to ponder and report upon the grim geographical realities of world politics. Authors such as the well known American commentator Thomas Barnett often claim, in a manner reminiscent of earlier geopolitical writers, an ability to see the world and to make confident predictions about its future composition, usually for the benefit of one particular country as opposed to others. Critical geopolitical writers aim to scrutinize those claims and, where appropriate, suggest other geographical ways of representing and understanding the world. This might include, for instance, laying emphasis on the human security and the gendered nature of global geopolitics, which often means that women and children are more vulnerable and exposed to geopolitical violence and geo-economic inequalities. Often this work attempts to liberate populations from oppressive geopolitical structures and promotes geographical understandings of a more equal world. This includes, for instance, laying greater emphasis on the gendered nature of global politics and geo-economic inequalities in the world trade system.

Chapter 3
Geopolitical architectures

In recent decades, the most important shorthand term used by political leaders, journalists, and academic commentators to describe and explain global political and economic change was globalization. Since the 1980s, it has become virtually hegemonic in academic and policy-making circles and was readily embraced by President Bill Clinton and Tony Blair in the 1990s, for example. Within those varied discussions, globalization was frequently assumed to be transforming the world around us, as governments and agencies such as the World Trade Organization, the United Nations, and the International Monetary Fund either encouraged or struggled to handle the apparent pace of change. As a consequence, territory and international borders appeared less significant in shaping human affairs—some commentators such as Richard O'Brien even referred to the 'End of Geography'. But things have changed in the last five years. Rather than subscribe to that view of globalization being an unqualified global good, this chapter will illustrate how globalization coexists with a geopolitical architecture involving states and other non-state bodies, which far from eroding the significance of borders and territory are contributing to dynamic and highly uneven reconfigurations. In the post-cold war era, the way we organize our world and define the roles and responsibilities of organizations such as the United Nations and the conduct of states has been subjected to intense scrutiny (see Box 6).

Box 6. Walls and security projects

One of the most powerful ways in which states register their determination to control or (attempt at least) to regulate mobility is by building walls and barriers. The wall may prevent the mobility of people and objects but it also might help to regulate—to slow down, to monitor, and ultimately control. However, walls and barricades can be circumvented, torn down, and ignored. Walls can also generate a 'black market' economy involving smugglers, crime syndicates, corrupt border officials, and citizens from all over the world trying to pass through such barriers. Many will fail, some will be seriously hurt, and others will die horribly in and around such borderlands. Some of the most prominent walls and barricades include the US–Mexico border and the West Bank security wall, which has been declared illegal and is widely seen as an attempt by the Israeli government to either colonize more territory and/or make Palestinian communities less sustainable. These walls and barriers stand in marked contrast to the ideas and practices associated with globalization with due emphasis given to mobility and exchange across borders. If anything, in the midst of a War on Terror, greater investment has been made in regulating and controlling the mobilities of people and objects but such activities are highly uneven as people living and working around these security walls learn to circumnavigate a coterie of official and unofficial security regulations and practices.

But what is globalization, before we consider more contemporary configurations? The term refers to the movement of people, ideas, technology, and goods from place to place with corresponding implications for human relations. Since the 15th and 16th centuries, these flows have become progressively more intense, often with severe implications for native populations in what were later to be described as the First, Second, and Third Worlds. The Dutch, Portuguese, Spanish, British, and French were at the forefront of this global enterprise and the 'colonial encounter' initiated a global trade in commodities and people including slaves. Global entities such as the Dutch East India Company, assisted by their imperial sponsors, helped to construct and administer these trading networks. By the 19th century, a new continental power, the United States, began to make its presence felt in terms of its flows of people, goods, and ideas alongside territorial acquisition in the Pacific Ocean and the Caribbean. As the global economy further materialized in the same period, the need for international coordination increased and the 1884 International Meridian Conference established Greenwich as the Prime Meridian and thus facilitated a new world map of agreed-upon time zones. The 20th century bore witness to even greater forms of social, political, and cultural connectivity due to the advances in aviation, automobiles, and containerization. At its end, as the international system widened and deepened, geography in the sense of physical space no longer seemed to matter. For the journalist Thomas Friedman, the year 2000 was the high water mark of globalization as software technology and the internet brought people and objects ever closer together (Figure 6).

6. The World Economic Forum Meeting at Davos, Switzerland. Russian conductor Vladimir Spivakov and the Moscow Virtuosi Chamber orchestra receive applause at the opening ceremony, 22 January 2013

While the 'End of Geography', like the 'End of History', has been much proclaimed, the varied geographies of globalization have arguably highlighted the significance of borders, distance, interconnection, and responsibilities. Since the 17th century, European states and later others such as the United States have sought actively to manage the relationship between national territories and accompanying flows of people, goods, ideas, and money. The 19th century, as Gerrit Gong has noted, heralded the establishment of 'standards of civilization' that enabled European states to determine the current and future shape of the international system and the criteria by which new states achieved legal recognition via a form of 'earned sovereignty'. The latter in its many and varied guises is an essential element of globalization as it helps to provide 'rules' and 'expectations' for the global order. The United States, as a great power, has in the recent past been at the forefront of establishing such an international legal order. It was instrumental in creating post-1945 institutions such as the United Nations and the 1948 Universal Declaration of Human Rights. In the United Nations Charter, for instance, states accept that the Security Council has the right to determine what constitutes threats to international peace and security and that states must comply with particular resolutions relating to these. More generally, there has been a gulf between legal sovereignty and de facto sovereignty in the sense that 'sovereignty' has been abused, divided, and shared. States also attempt to protect and conserve their 'sovereignty' whether it involves building barriers, restricting mobilities, or engaging in territorial aggression against others.

The notion of 'abuse' is significant because in the last five years we have witnessed increased evidence that citizens around the world have taken to the streets to protest about a particular geopolitical architecture, combining neo-liberal globalization and security. In late 2010, protestors in Tunisia precipitated a social movement, later dubbed the 'Arab Spring', which was credited with provoking regime change (or the threat of) across the Middle East. At the

51

same time, social movements, such as the 'Occupy Movement', were also increasingly active around the world highlighting what they called the '99%' of citizens who are being excluded from the associated benefits of globalization. Far from being a straightforward 'public good', contemporary forms of globalization, often described as neo-liberal, were perceived to be beneficial to business and government elites, especially in highly stratified societies such as the United States and United Kingdom, but not exclusively so. At its height the Occupy Movement was credited with stimulating protests in over 80 countries and 900 cities (Figure 7). The onset of a severe financial crisis and recession

7. The Occupy London Movement at St Paul's Cathedral, October 2011–February 2012

(2007–8 onwards) added further resonance to these protests as governments began to promote the politics of austerity and retrenchment.

The term *geopolitical architecture* is used to describe the ways in which states and non-state organizations access, manage, and regulate the intersection of territories and flows and in so doing establish borders between inside/outside, citizen/alien, and domestic/international. Historically speaking, there have been a series of such geopolitical architectures which re-jig the relationship between spaces and flows. Governments, for instance, invest greatly in the regulation of borders as they provide the entry/exit point into a national territory. Such border controls also become a significant element in demonstrating effective sovereignty. In order to understand those shifts and the implications for geopolitical theorizing, we need to consider two fundamental subjects—first, the term sovereignty and how it informs the activities of the state and, second, the geopolitical architecture of the 20th and now the early 21st centuries, which highlights how states in particular attempt to control and regulate spaces judged to be disorderly and ungoverned.

National sovereignty and the international system

The ideas and practices associated with sovereignty are critical in shaping the prevailing geopolitical architecture based on states, borders, and national territories. As Stephen Krasner has noted, national governments, while endorsing the importance of sovereignty, have frequently violated those ideas and principles as incorporated into the founding charter of the United Nations. Apart from high-profile invasions of countries, state authorities frequently spy, survey, and carry out covert operations that violate the territorial sovereignty of other states. The United States has a worldwide spying and surveillance capacity thanks to specialist agencies such as the National Security Agency and CIA. Governments willingly allow their national sovereignty to be violated by encouraging certain flows of investment, skilled people, and ideas. Since the enlargement of the European Union, the British government has encouraged labour migration from countries such as Poland and Slovakia. In other cases, governments may appeal for humanitarian and/or military intervention when faced with overwhelming evidence of human rights violation and suffering. Sometimes governments might express outrage at sovereignty violations while secretly encouraging such an arrangement. US drone strikes in Pakistan might fall into such a category and the 'outrage' being expressed is thus directed towards the domestic citizenry being affected.

In thinking about sovereignty, as a key building block of geopolitical architecture, it is helpful to distinguish four different types of interpretation. First, commentators frequently refer to the international legal manifestations of sovereignty in the form of membership of the United Nations, the ability to negotiate and ratify treaties alongside the general business associated with diplomacy. At the heart of these activities is the notion that states recognize other states and therefore accept that they have an inherent capacity to conduct *international* relations. Even if other governments detest a state and its political leadership, that basic recognition is fundamental. In the weeks and months leading up to the 2003 invasion of Iraq, the United States and its allies had to negotiate and engage with Saddam Hussein's diplomatic representatives in the United Nations. In other cases, some states might not recognize the capacity of other states to conduct international relations precisely because they are considered to be unable to manage their national territories let alone engage with the wider world. Terms such as 'failing states' and 'quasi-states' have been used to imply that some countries in regions such as West and Central Africa can neither claim exclusive control over their territory nor secure internal order. In other words, Western governments frequently represent states such as Somalia and/or the Democratic Republic of Congo as inadequate and, moreover, unable to regulate flows of drugs, money, and arms trafficking. It is important to recall, however, that some of the earliest geopolitical writers such as Kjellen objected to this excessively legalistic conception of sovereignty precisely because it neglected the fact that the geographies of global politics were extremely varied. So terms such as 'failing state' acknowledge in part that the capacities of states vary even if they enjoy similar international recognition to others.

Second, we might consider sovereignty as conditioned by interdependence. In an era of intense globalization, it is unhelpful to presume that states enjoy exclusive control over their territories and accompanying flows with associated levels of mobility. Even the most powerful countries in the world such as the United States and China have had to recognize, in their different ways, that interdependence, while it has not eroded state sovereignty completely, has nonetheless modified politics and policy making. In some areas of social life, such as those encapsulated by national security, countries have attempted to respond to interdependence by enhancing governmental and, in the case of the 27 European Union parties, regional control in the form of immigration control and surveillance while sharing or even conceding formal sovereignty in areas such as human rights protection and economic cooperation. This is sometimes referred to as 'pooling sovereignty'.

Third, we might consider sovereignty in purely domestic terms and recognize some states are better able than others to exercise control over their national territories. Comparing the United States with the Democratic Republic of Congo would be stark, as the latter has been consumed by a series of conflicts since the late 1990s, which have led to the death of millions, the mass rape of women and girls, and the destruction of villages. The national government based in Kinshasa does not exercise effective control over its large territory and this emboldened other countries to contribute to instability by funding rival militias. During the cold war, the country previously named Zaire was governed by the plutocratic regime headed by Mobutu (1965–97) and was tolerated by others such as the United States because it was regarded as a vital anti-communist ally in Central Africa. Mobutu was able to maintain some form of domestic sovereignty over the country because he used his well-funded armed forces (supported by exports in minerals and oil) to quell any form of resistance and unrest. This changed after his death in 1997 while in exile in Morocco.

However, even powerful countries such as the United States with well-established infrastructures and administrative structures struggle to exercise complete sovereign control. The control of immigration is one such issue, especially with regard to the US–Mexican border, which continues to pose problems for the federal authorities. The US Border Patrol, despite additional investment in personnel, vehicles, and sensory equipment, struggles on a daily basis to regulate the movement of people across the Rio Grande and desert regions of South-Western America. In light of these difficulties, American citizens have created vigilante groups such as the Minuteman Project to patrol and pursue those who are intent on illegally entering the United States. This group, however, is not simply concerned with immigration but voices concerns over the status of Anglophone America and the growing challenge posed by Spanish-speaking communities in the South-West.

Fourth, other parties when respecting the principle of non-intervention explicitly recognize sovereignty. Developed by the Swiss jurist Emmerich de Vattel, the idea that states should be able to conduct their own affairs without intervention from outside powers is a vital ingredient of the current political architecture. For states emerging from the shadow of European colonialism, this was particularly significant in facilitating the creation of post-colonial governments. However, American and Soviet administrations frequently interfered in the affairs of other countries, especially those in the so-called Third World, whether in the form of military invasions, economic blockades, cultural penetration, political marginalization, and/or sanctions. For example, the United States invaded the Dominican Republic in 1965 and destabilized Chile in 1973 because it feared the emergence of further socialist governments in the Americas following the successful consolidation of the 1959 Cuban Revolution associated with the leadership of Fidel Castro. The Soviets sent tanks into Budapest in 1956 and again into Prague in 1968 in order to crush reformist governments. The underlying impulse of the cold war geopolitical architecture was one of spatial containment, seeking thus to restrict the mobility of people, ideas, and objects especially if originating (in the US case) from the Soviet Union and its allies.

In other areas of international life, many states have actively encouraged the qualification of the principle of non-intervention, as developments in human rights protection would seem to testify. The international community as represented by the United Nations' permanent members has not always responded so readily to evidence of massive human rights violation and genocide in some places such as Darfur (Sudan) despite agitation from pressure groups, celebrities such as George Clooney, and other states outside of the region.

Some states are better able to exercise effective sovereignty in the sense that they claim a capacity to control and administer their national territories and regulate flows of money, people, goods, ideas, and/or technology. Others possess greater extraterritorial capacities such as the United States and China and are able thus to conduct genuinely globalized relations. This capacity to interfere and engage with other states, other communities, and other regions was of course recognized by some of the earliest geopolitical thinkers. The post-Columbian era, as Halford Mackinder noted, was likely to be characterized by more intense relationships as states recognized that the world was being compressed by new technologies including transportation.

Time-space compression has become even more intense and the term globalization has been widely used to encapsulate those shifts in the human experience notwithstanding the arguments over its geographical intensity and significance.

Geopolitical architecture in an age of intense globalization

If we want to understand more fully how global geopolitics has changed since Mackinder's era, then we need to examine how states, amongst others, have responded, resisted, and regulated processes associated with globalization. If traditional geopolitical thinking was preoccupied with states and the changing fortunes of European empires, then more recent writings have explored the role of non-state actors, networks, regional organizations, transnational corporations, and international governmental organizations. While states and concepts such as sovereignty remain highly significant, a web of interdependence is changing international relations and accompanying global geographies. It is now common to read that states possess permeable borders and that governance is expressed in a more global and polycentric manner, as institutions such as the World Bank, the United Nations, global media corporations, and the World Trade Organization play their parts in shaping global behaviour.

The notion of intensity is important here because of mounting evidence that states have had to adapt to ever more issues and flows that possess an ability to transcend international boundaries and exclusive sovereignties. The list would undoubtedly include global climate change, human rights, drug trafficking, and the spectre of nuclear annihilation. Over the last 60 years, a particular form of global order was said to have prevailed following the defeat of Japan and Germany in 1945. Sponsored by the victorious United States and its allies including Britain, it has been characterized by three key features—the development of a global capitalist economy, the creation of the United Nations, and the promotion of liberal democracy. The United States was instrumental in creating a new economic order based on the creation of two institutions: the International Monetary Fund (IMF) and the World Bank. These bodies, first considered at Bretton Woods, New Hampshire, in 1944, would aim to establish international economic stability and provide funds for post-war reconstruction (Box 7).

Box 7. Bretton Woods: the ending of an international economic order?

The Bretton Woods system of international monetary management was intended to establish the rules governing post-war commercial and financial relations. The spectre of aggressive forms of economic nationalism was to be banished in the process. At the heart of this system were 44 nations who attended the United Nations Monetary and Financial Conference in July 1944. Once it had been ratified in 1946, each country had to accept that the exchange rate of its currency would remain within a fixed value banding so that the International Monetary Fund could help promote and manage global financial stability. In 1971, the system of fixed currencies collapsed and the United States suspended the conversion from dollars to gold.

After 1971, international currencies were no longer tied to particular exchange rates and international financial flows increased. A number of world cities, such as New York, Paris, and London, emerged as major hubs of the post-Bretton Woods era.

Second, the creation of the United Nations in 1945 was instrumental in helping to manage and regulate the behaviour of states in the post-war world. The United Nations Charter played a key role in establishing sovereignty norms as well as other interventions such as the General Agreement of Tariffs and Trade, which sought to promote global free trade. Third, the promotion of liberal democracy by the United States as the preferred system of political expression was critical in legitimating their role in the ensuing cold war struggle involving the Soviet Union and China who publicly promoted socialist revolutions. As a consequence of the collapse of the Soviet Union in 1991 and the decline of socialist regimes in Eastern Europe and elsewhere, institutions associated with the economic and political imprint of the United States have effectively prefigured and advocated the prioritization of global capitalist development based on free trade, open markets, and foreign direct investment (Box 8). Transnational corporations have facilitated the consolidation of such a global economic landscape through their investment and production activities.

Box 8. From Yalta to Berlin: the overturning of European political boundaries

In February 1945, the Soviet Union, the United States, and Britain participated in a meeting in the Crimean resort of Yalta. This conference, involving Stalin, Roosevelt, and Churchill, effectively determined the fate of post-1945 Europe. The main outcomes were: the Soviet Union would join the United Nations in return for a buffer zone in Eastern and Central Europe; the Soviets would declare war on Japan; Germany and Austria would be occupied and divided into four sectors and managed by the three conference participants plus France; Germany would have to pay reparations; and countries such as Estonia and Latvia were allowed to remain under Soviet occupation.

It would take another 44 years before the geopolitics of Europe was to be fundamentally altered by the collapse of the East German regime and other communist governments in Eastern and Central Europe. The break-up of the Berlin Wall (built in 1961) was one of the most memorable moments of that transformation. By the end of the 1990s, the Soviet Union had disintegrated, former Eastern European communist governments had joined the European Union (EU) and the North Atlantic Treaty Organization (NATO), and Russia had formed new partnerships with both the EU and NATO.

The ramifications for the state in an era of intense globalization have been much debated. For some, the state has been eclipsed by these intense demands of the global economic and political order. Economic institutions such as the World Bank and IMF are able, especially in sub-Saharan Africa and Asia, to exercise considerable control over government expenditure and macro-economic policy where and when states have requested financial assistance. So-called structural adjustment programmes (SAP) have imposed accompanying conditions, which might include demands that governments cut public expenditure or ease restrictions on foreign investment. During the cold war, such international economic arrangements had geopolitical implications as US-dominated international organizations such as the IMF rendered greater control and influence over regions, such as West Africa, considered to be strategically significant because of their natural oil and natural gas resources. Marxist geographer David Harvey has referred to 'accumulation by dispossession' to highlight the manner in which international institutions have facilitated access to Third World markets and resources. In other regions of the world such as South-East Asia, international loans were directed towards states considered to be allies in the struggle against Soviet and/or Chinese-backed socialist ambitions. Countries such as South Korea and Malaysia were the beneficiaries in this regard, especially during the Vietnam conflict. American administrators in particular feared that if Vietnam fell to communist forces then other neighbouring countries would also be vulnerable to socialist interference.

Other commentators contend that international economic organizations such as the IMF or transnational corporations depend on their relationship with states, albeit one that has been transformed by global flows and networks. States ultimately created the post-war economic and political order and the United States was the most significant in this regard. Moreover, property, taxation, and investment laws both regulate and protect the activities of transnational corporations. The notion of a 'transformed state' is more helpful in the sense that it can be used to highlight in which ways globalization has altered the 'state of affairs' including global political order. As the economic geographer Peter Dicken has opined, states continue to shape specific business and economic activities and regulate within and across their national jurisdictions. Ironically, there are now more states than ever, at a time when some observers have predicted the demise of the state as a direct consequence of intense globalization.

The implications for geopolitics are profound. On the one hand, the ending of the cold war witnessed new states and regional organizations such as Slovenia and the Commonwealth of Independent States (CIS) respectively. The collapse of the Soviet Union and the gradual incorporation of Russia and China into international economic bodies such as the World Trade Organization (WTO) have highlighted how former communist/socialist countries are embedded within the networks and structures associated with global capitalist development. Along with widespread democratization in Eastern Europe, Latin America, and parts of Asia and Africa, policies associated with neo-liberalism such as open markets and foreign direct investment are hegemonic. A deregulated vision of world geography has prevailed—the globe as a border-free zone, which encourages flows of investment and goods. The state was intended to be a facilitator of business and some large US-based companies such as Enron were, at one point, well able to take full advantage of the relative lack of judicial and fiscal structures. During the 1990s, commentators such as Francis Fukuyama lauded the triumph of these ideas and practices associated with US-sponsored neo-liberalism and democracy.

On the other hand, it was also obvious that democracy in the form of free elections and elected representatives was not the norm in all parts of the world including China, sub-Saharan Africa, and parts of the Islamic world. Even when democracy has appeared in places such as Egypt and Algeria, for instance, it has been not been welcomed by all citizens and interest groups including the militaries of those countries. Moreover, even those countries considered by some to be democratic were radically different to Western European and American models. The ever-greater adoption of economic neo-liberalism has attracted a great deal of opposition in many countries in the Third World as well as Western Europe and the United States. The emergence of an anti-globalization movement is perhaps one of the most obvious manifestations of that resistance to the hegemonic presence of the United States and its advocated forms of neo-liberal global order. This movement, which is incredibly diverse, is often described as 'new' because these bodies appeal to transboundary communities and thus seek to subvert a world based on bounded territories and international frontiers. These groupings frequently do not seek to establish formal political representation in any one country.

The most high-profile anti-globalization demonstrations occurred in cities such as Cologne, Genoa, London, and Seattle. Frequently coinciding with meetings of the WTO or G8, anti-globalization critics are censorious of the way neo-liberalism has eroded national boundaries and thus exposed communities to unwanted interference from global corporations, international institutions, and/or hegemonic powers. At its heart lies the concern that certain kinds of flows are overwhelming local places and communities and that national governments are not able or willing to mitigate those flows as they intersect with territories. Arguably one of the most dramatic examples of anti-globalization endeavour occurred in Seattle in November 1999. Timed to coincide with a WTO meeting, 60,000 people descended on the Pacific Coast city to register their grievances against corporate globalization and compelled the United States to use its military forces in order to restore civic order. The protests continued around the world and in 2001 a World Social Forum was established in Brazil to consolidate and coordinate resistance to these neo-liberal forms of globalization. Over 100,000 people attended Forum meetings in India and Brazil in 2004 and 2005 respectively.

The anti-globalization movement remains diverse and although now partly preoccupied with other anti-war movements in resisting the War on Terror and the occupation of Iraq, its activities have contested and disrupted the existing neo-liberal economic and political order. Such initiatives were bolstered further by the initiation of the Occupy Movement, which was launched in October 2011 as an international protest movement against socio-economic inequality (Box 9). Inspired by the 'Arab Spring' movement and the Indignados Movement in Spain and

Box 9. Placing protest: Zuccotti Park, New York City

Zuccotti Park, or Liberty Plaza Park, would have been unknown to most citizens except New Yorkers and visitors to that city. Located in Lower Manhattan, it was damaged in the midst of the 11 September 2001 attack on the Twin Towers. Renamed after the park was bought by a corporation in 2006, it had hosted a series of commemorative events in the months and years after 9/11. A decade later, Zuccotti Park was the site of an altogether different kind of geopolitical performance, one in which the city of New York (and the United States) was not being remembered as a victim of violence but as a producer of inequality around the world. On 17 September 2011, protestors gathered at Zuccotti Park to launch 'Occupy Wall Street'. The choice of the location was not only close to New York's financial centre but also well chosen in the sense of being a privately owned park that could not be shut down by the city authorities. The park's owners, Brookfield Properties, the City of New York government, and the New York Police Department then found themselves locked in a series of legal and physical battles to restrict access to the park and prevent the erection of tents and installations in the park itself. Such restrictions remain in place to this day but the protests provoked national and international debate, and high-profile individuals such as Naomi Wolf were arrested while expressing support for the protestors.

Portugal, there was growing interest in registering widespread protest against the concentration of global wealth and the corporatization of global geopolitics. The word 'Occupy' was important because this was a highly geographical protest movement. Whilst its aim was to call for a recalibration of neo-liberal globalization and the interaction of the international financial system, it was also a spatial challenge. In the same month, protestors established a protest camp outside St Paul's Cathedral in the City of London. The choice was a deliberate one. The proximity to the financial centre of London was intended to highlight the close relationship between the UK government and the international banking sector, but also to ask questions about what role civil society and the third sector (including religious organizations) should play in the midst of financial crisis and austerity.

Neo-liberal globalization, War on Terror, and 'broken windows'

How might neo-liberal globalization be connected to the War on Terror? Some commentators have suggested that the analogy of 'broken windows' might help explain such a link. While neo-liberal globalization intensifies, with governments such as the US and UK giving ever-greater emphasis to market accessibility and tax-friendly policies for business coupled with reduced state involvement in the public sector, the War on Terror also precipitated increased expenditure in military/security sectors. As a result, concern has been expressed that the distinction between the domestic and the international is increasingly being blurred by transnational security practices, which aim to secure economic and political spaces in the City of London and Wall Street and in places such as Afghanistan and Iraq. In other words, there is a growing interest in how people, regardless of location per se, are policed and securitized. Of course, places still matter in the sense that the nature and extent of that policing and security work does vary and some bodies will be made more precarious than others but in general is globalization becoming more akin to a global security project (Box 10)?

Box 10. Did President Obama (secretly) support the Occupy Movement?

Let's remember how we got here. Long before the recession, jobs and manufacturing began leaving our shores. Technology made businesses more efficient, but also made some jobs obsolete. Folks at the top saw their incomes rise like never before, but most hardworking Americans struggled with costs that were growing, paychecks that weren't, and personal debt that kept piling up.

In 2008, the house of cards collapsed. We learned that mortgages had been sold to people who couldn't afford or understand them. Banks had made huge bets and bonuses with other people's money. Regulators had looked the other way, or didn't have the authority to stop the bad behavior.

It was wrong. It was irresponsible. And it plunged our economy into a crisis that put millions out of work, saddled us with more debt, and left innocent, hardworking Americans holding the bag. In the six months before I took office, we lost nearly 4 million jobs. And we lost another 4 million before our policies were in full effect.

President Barrack Obama 2012 State of the Union Address

Social scientists, in political geography and allied fields such as International Relations and Security Studies, argue that the current geopolitical architecture is predicated on spatial administration rather than containment. So securing neo-liberal globalization is thus rendered dependent on more intense forms of intervention into the lives of citizens around the world. One suggestion is that terms like 'broken windows', originally used to justify and legitimate the reform of urban life in 1980s and 1990s New York, are being used more generally to argue for more governance, embracing surveillance and policing. In the original New York contest, the idea was that any form of criminal behaviour needed to be tackled, such as graffiti. If city authorities failed to tackle the 'little things' then criminals would think that 'bigger things' such as robbery and violent assault would not be pursued. The 'broken window' had to be taken seriously.

This analogy is profoundly spatial. There were areas of the city that needed greater governance including, in the New York context, the subway. However, the analogy was also powerful because it highlighted flow and mobility as well. People were responsible for those 'broken windows' and they had to be tracked and prosecuted. Worse still a failure to act in one area of the city might encourage other areas to also experience their own 'broken windows'. So 'weak states' and 'thinly governed' territories even in places like New York are disturbing precisely because they might act to unsettle and disrupt other areas. From the streets of New Orleans, in the aftermath of Hurricane Katrina in 2005, to the alleyways of Baghdad, the juxtaposition of broken windows/zero tolerance is said to have enabled new kinds of business and security practice, which Naomi Klein claims empowers corporations and states to invest, intervene, and regulate through policing, taxation, and surveillance. Post-invasion Iraq was rapidly turned into a business-security opportunity for countless corporations and companies including Halliburton, Bechtel, and Blackwater. And cities such as New York and London were made safer and more business friendly, including for tourists and visitors.

Longer term, we appear to be witnessing the hybridization of two kinds of geopolitical architectures—on the one hand, predicated on spatial containment (as epitomized by the War on Terror and the invasion and subjugation of weak or threatening states) and on the other hand, one underpinned by spatial administration. Neo-liberal globalization, with due emphasis on market accessibility and privatization, encourages both variants. The invasions of Afghanistan and Iraq were both acts of spatial containment (to prevent the spread of further terror operations) and acts of spatial administration (to reform populations and states). And as the 11 September 2001 attacks revealed to US business and government elites, the interaction of flows, networks, and mobility, championed in the 1990s, was now seen in the early part of the 21st century as inherently more threatening and disconcerting.

What is likely to emerge in the future is emphasis being placed on spatial administration, the idea being, as we are already witnessing now, intervention on the part of state and trusted partners in a range of sites and spaces. This has domestic and external implications. Domestically, as the state retreats increasingly from public sector provision it is likely to expand in areas such as policing and surveillance. Poor urban communities will bear the brunt of this intervention because it is they who are most likely to be judged to be detrimental to the business of the state. New technologies and data (e.g. 'big data' and machine learning techniques) will facilitate further intervention often in the name of more efficient governance. Populations become increasingly surveyed and targeted depending on demographic and socio-economic trending. Externally, places lacking strong governance are likely to be increasingly seen as threatening to the prevailing geopolitical architecture: places like Afghanistan, which act to incubate threats, or even the US inner city, which is represented as an under-governed space.

Conclusions

A word that we are likely to hear more of in the future is 'resilience'. If analogies to 'broken windows' and appeals to 'austerity' continue then this will have implications for how geopolitical architectures impact upon the everyday lives of citizens. As neo-liberalism intensifies, despite the protests following the global financial crisis and its impact on citizens around the world, so pressure continues to be exerted on governments and states to reduce their public spending and make themselves ever more attractive and accessible to global investment and business. In the United Kingdom and the United States, for example, this has led to pressure on governments to reign in spending and to encourage citizens to develop more resilient strategies, placing the onus on them to better prepare themselves for further crises and disruption. Within continental Europe there has been angry reaction from civil society regarding such public sector retrenchment and appeals for citizen resilience. Countries such as Greece, caught up in complex financial restrictions involving European Union institutions, have witnessed widespread protesting and deepening poverty such that the charitable sector has had to step into the gaps left by the retreating state. Compounding such retraction and austerity, regional geopolitical transformation in North Africa has encouraged greater migration, via the Mediterranean, to countries such as Italy, Malta, and Greece, in so doing revealing some of the essential features of the prevailing geopolitical architecture as it seeks, through governments and international institutions, to regulate flows and territories.

Chapter 4
Geopolitics and identity

One way to assess the importance of identity politics to geopolitics is to think of examples where this is brought into sharp relief. When do claims to national identity get stress tested, and critically where? In February 2012, a feminist punk rock group called Pussy Riot staged a live performance at the Moscow Cathedral of Christ the Saviour. The group, established in August 2011, is composed of a group of young women who compose and perform songs that address feminism, gay rights, and contemporary social and political policies of Russian President Vladimir Putin. They are particularly scathing of the connections between the Russian government and the Orthodox Church and contend that the two sustain a politically and culturally repressive culture, which oppresses citizens judged to threaten national ideals. Most people outside Russia had not heard of Pussy Riot and would not have done so had three not been arrested in March 2012 after their live performance at the Moscow Cathedral. The group members involved were charged with 'hooliganism' and accused of stirring religious hatred.

The sentencing of the musicians attracted widespread criticism and was perceived as an overreaction by the Russian authorities. President Putin at the time accused the women of undermining the 'moral foundations' of the nation. The controversy of their imprisonment is interesting for students of geopolitics not only because of its spatial dimensions (the performance at the Moscow Cathedral was regarded as particularly provocative as was the dispatch of the women to penal colonies associated with the Soviet era Gulag system) but also its imaginative dimension. At the heart of the case was a sense that this punk band was guilty of transgression. Their songs were judged to violate the moral integrity of the state by mocking the president and the credibility of presidential elections. More recently, the Russian government has come under renewed scrutiny about how it treats gay and lesbian citizens and environmental campaigners, and the manner in which legal charges such as 'hooliganism' are used to stifle dissent within Russia. In a desire to protect a 'strong national identity' does contemporary Russia rely on an exclusionary geopolitical and cultural imagination, which positions some people and groups as unwelcome, illegal, and/or threatening?

This chapter grapples with some of the issues raised by terms such as national identity and argues that an essential element of geopolitical theorizing is preoccupied with this subject. National identity has to be constructed and historians have been at the forefront of noting how national traditions and traits are invented. The making and remaking of national identities is a creative process and also inherently geographical because they are associated with particular places. Identity narratives are not of course restricted simply to the level of the nation state but can and do operate at a variety of geographical scales from the subnational to the pan-regional and finally to the global. Examples to be explored in this chapter include the European Union and other regional organizations and the manner in which other cultural and political groupings such as subnational groupings, social movements, and diaspora challenge particular claims to national identity. As the capacities of states to control their economic, cultural, and political space has been challenged by non-state actors and associated flows, so those claims to exclusive national identities have often become all the more urgent (and potentially dangerous).

Geopolitics and national identity

The creation of the modern international political system based on national states with exclusive territorial jurisdictions is commonly dated to 17th-century Europe. Over the ensuing centuries, national governments emerged and established via diplomacy and international law, a mosaic of states which has now encompassed the earth's surface with the exception of Antarctica and parts of the oceans. As the apparatus of the state began to envelop the everyday affairs of citizens, national governments through their control and/or monitoring of national media and/or school-level education began to concentrate ever-greater energy in the creation and maintenance of a national self-identity.

In the case of Argentina, for instance, which declared independence from the Spanish Empire in 1810, this was considered an essential element in the survival of the nation state. The process of creating what Benedict Anderson has called an 'imagined community' took several forms, one of which was the introduction of so-called 'patriotic education' in the late 19th century to generate a national consciousness. The timing of these educational reforms was not accidental; the government of Buenos Aires had not only extended its sovereign authority over a more extensive geographical territory, including the most southerly region of Patagonia, but also had to contend with new waves of immigrants primarily from Italy and Spain who had to be incorporated and inculcated with a sense of what it was to be an Argentine citizen.

In the regional context of South America, territorial boundaries remained a highly sensitive affair, as countries such as Argentina, Chile, Bolivia, Paraguay, and Brazil negotiated, often with the assistance of nascent national armies, national territories and border regions. This process was largely beneficial for Argentina as it expanded southwards, westwards, and northwards. Others, such as Paraguay, were less fortunate. The so-called War of the

Triple Alliance (1864–70) led to a disastrous outcome. Paraguay lost territory and perhaps over 50 per cent of its adult population to a series of wars with Argentina, Brazil, and Uruguay. In the case of land-locked Bolivia, the so-called War of the Pacific involving others such as Chile and Peru, led to the loss of a territorial corridor to the Pacific Ocean. While Argentina would be considered a territorial success story by comparison with Bolivia and Paraguay, one event in the 19th century was to have a dramatic impact on subsequent expressions of national identity and purpose—the loss of the Islas Malvinas to the British in 1833.

One of the most important elements of future patriotic education was the geographical lesson that Argentina was an incomplete country. Later described as the 'Lost Little Sisters', the annexation of these South-West Atlantic islands continues to grate and remains an integral element in expressions of Argentine national identity. School-level education continues to promote this view and ensures that every young school child can draw an outline of the two main islands (East and West Falkland according to English speakers) at primary level. As the reference to 'Lost Little Sisters' suggests, the territory is often described in highly gendered terms; as a sisterly appendage of the body politic, which is continental Argentina (the Fatherland). It is not surprising, therefore, that when the Falklands were 'invaded' by Argentine forces in 1982, the action was vindicated as an act of geographical salvation after an earlier 'rape' by perfidious Albion. Remarkably for non-Argentine audiences, crowds gathering in the main square proximate to the so-called Pink House in Buenos Aires cheered the military regime. At the same time, this and other military governments in the recent past were torturing and executing their own citizens. Geographical indoctrination seemed so complete that many in the Republic were willing, at that moment, to celebrate this act of territorial annexation.

The British victory in June 1982 did not resolve this particular territorial crisis. Despite the claims to the contrary by the

Thatcher government, Argentine citizens continue to be informed that this territorial grievance remains outstanding. I recall my first visit to Argentina, on the tenth anniversary of the conflict, and quite how that geographical sensibility endured. If the British were content to commemorate the conflict as something located in the recent past (and at the same time as connected to older British victories such as the Second World War), Argentine media organizations and governments encouraged citizens and indeed visitors to imagine this territorial dispute as ongoing. If you opened a magazine and examined weather reports for the Republic, you would have noticed that the Falklands were labelled as the Malvinas and thus indisputably Argentine. Since the late 1940s, it has been an offence in Argentina to produce any map of the Republic that did not label the Falklands as Argentine and for that matter a portion of the Antarctic closest to the South American mainland. Public maps and murals constantly remind the citizen and visitor that the islands are geographically proximate to Patagonia. British sovereignty is constantly condemned not only as reminiscent of earlier episodes of imperialism but also indicative of a particularly distasteful form of geographical overstretch. Since 1982, public war monuments in Buenos Aires and elsewhere also provide a further opportunity for geographical and cultural reflection on what they consider should be Argentine national territory.

This apparent obsession with the recovery of the Falkland Islands has broader implications for Argentine national identity. On the one hand, it shaped a particular view of the Republic as a geographically violated country, which remains highly sensitive to territorial matters, as immediate neighbours such as Chile would attest. Both countries have argued for much of their histories over their Andean territorial boundary. This has sometimes resulted in seemingly farcical situations in which both sides argue over remote, unpopulated territorial fragments. On the other hand, the UK's annexation of the Falklands in the 19th century allowed later government leaders such as President

Perón in the 1940s and 1950s to construct a national vision for Argentina as a country eager to dispense with British and other imperial influence. This continues today as more recent presidents such as Christina Kirchner rail against continued British control of the Islands and look upon future oil and gas development with considerable concern. New revenue streams, combined with an increasingly confident Falkland Islands government (which organized a high-profile referendum on its future in March 2013) make it less and less likely that the UK will ever negotiate.

Argentina's territorial obsessions are not unique and similar stories could be told for other countries such as India and Pakistan, which as a result of partition have had to endure conflicts over northern territories. In all three countries, maps are extremely sensitive in terms of what they depict with regards either to national boundaries and/or territorial ownership. Territorial anxieties also help to shape school curricula and broader self-understandings. The national media in that respect can be extremely significant in not only generating a sense of 'imagined community' but also helping to cement particular self-understandings. As the political theorist William Connolly has noted, 'Identity requires difference in order to be, and it converts difference into otherness in order to secure its own self-certainty'. In Argentina, it is common to read, view, and listen to stories about the disputed ownership of the Falklands and the threat posed by British imperialism. Further visual reminders are provided by seemingly banal objects such as stamps, tea towels, signposts, and badges embossed with the simple claim: the Malvinas are Argentine. In this and other highly territorialized cultures, claims to particular forms of national identity are rooted and resolved by evoking the spectre of British imperialism. The geopolitics of national identity is pronounced in countries such as Argentina because territorial grievances and uncertainties over international boundaries are held to jeopardize claims to national identity.

In other countries such as the United States, which have successfully expanded with little direct experience of territorial loss, national identity formation has taken on a different expression. If Argentines worry about their territorial portfolio, Americans have been largely preoccupied with the social and racial character of their national community. The experiences of such as the Native American, Japanese American, and African-American communities stand in sharp contrast to the experiences of white Protestant Americans, who continue to shape the prevailing political culture of that country. The political geography of the United States has been profoundly shaped by struggles for other minorities to be recognized by the national polity. The civil rights movements of the 1950s and 1960s and the fight to secure civil liberties for African-American communities occurred against the geopolitical backdrop of the cold war. While Rosa Parks and her fellow protestors in Montgomery, Alabama, were struggling to secure her right to occupy a bus seat, the Eisenhower administration was engaged in a titanic struggle with the Soviet Union for the hearts and minds of the world.

If America defined itself by championing liberty and freedom, many African-Americans must have choked on the tragic irony— while American presidents sought to defend freedoms elsewhere, communities inside the United States were being disenfranchised, degraded, and denigrated. So national symbols such as the Statue of Liberty can be interpreted in different ways depending on, for example, community experiences. African-American communities located in cities such as New Orleans, in the aftermath of Hurricane Katrina, made similar politico-geographical connections as it became clear that the federal government had been slow to react to the loss of life and property of the poor and the immobile. African-American families were over-represented in both categories.

Another contemporary example, following 9/11, would be the apparently ambivalent role occupied by the Arab-American and the Asian-American communities. Judged by their appearance and skin colour, many Arab-Americans and people of South Asian origin have complained of being subjected to harassment, intimidation, and frequent ejections from scheduled flights because other passengers complained about their demeanour and choice of language—Arabic or Urdu rather than English for instance. As a consequence, the Council of Arab-American Relations has complained that the community feels victimized and stigmatized because of the actions of 15 Saudi and 4 other Arabic-speaking hijackers on 11 September 2001. Far from being inconsequential, this has led to the suggestion that America's War on Terror is leading to new forms of identity politics that prioritize certain expressions of gender, race, and sexuality largely at the expense of ethnic minorities who are now viewed with fear and loathing, especially if they occupy public and confined spaces such as aircrafts, ships, and trains. Even comic-book heroes such as Captain America now battle it out with Islamic terrorists who are depicted as assaulting Christian-American values in imaginary towns such as Centreville.

Identity and territory have frequently enriched one another in the context of nation states. National territories have functioned as seemingly stable platforms for the manufacturing and reproduction of national identities. Institutions such as the national media and education system have and continue to provide the capacity to generate particular representations of national communities as territorially incomplete (Argentina), territorially violated (Palestine), territorially aspirant (Palestine, Kosovo, and Kurdistan), territorially ambitious (China), and as an example to the wider world (the United States) (see Box 11).

Box 11. Facebook and Kosovo

In November 2013, the social network company Facebook decided to list Kosovo as if it was an independent country (following on from the 2008 Declaration of Independence which is not recognized by Serbia). Prior to that point, Kosovars had to choose 'Serbia' if they wished to establish a Facebook account. It is estimated that some 200,000 users of Facebook were transferred from 'Serbia' or possibly 'Albania' to 'Kosovo'. The Kosovo prime minister was apparently told in advance by the social media company of their decision to acknowledge 'Kosovo' as an approved location. Interestingly, members of the Kosovo government were quick to recognize this decision as a positive contribution to Kosovo's public relations and commitment to join the European Union. While Facebook has never claimed to enjoy the power to 'recognize' countries in the way that sovereign states and the United Nations do (and some 100 countries have already recognized Kosovo as an independent state), it does highlight how the digital diplomacy of states including Kosovo is partly shaped by an interest in the behaviour of social media corporations. It is worth recalling that over 1 billion people are estimated to be active Facebook users so this kind of digital recognition of Kosovo will be welcomed by key Kosovo sectors such as government, business, and tourism, although it is unlikely to be welcomed by the Serbian government and those within Kosovo opposed to independence.

Geopolitics and pan-regional identity

National expressions of identity are arguably still the most significant, given the prevailing international political system based on nation states and territorial boundaries. However, identities are not always territorially bounded. Sometimes identities can simply leak beyond particular territorial boundaries or be deliberately produced so that they transcend the existing mosaic of states and their national boundaries. Europe provides one such example and the 1957 Treaty of Rome and its antecedents are significant in this regard. Scarred by the experiences of devastating world wars, European political figures particularly in France and Germany, such as Jean Monnet and Konrad Adenauer, were instrumental in initiating a political, economic, social, and cultural process designed to promote European cooperation and eventual integration. For West Germany, recovering from the losses imposed by two global conflicts and territorial partition, the Treaty of Rome was not just about promoting European integration, it was also further evidence that the country sought to reimagine itself as an integral part of a democratic Europe and, as it turned out, a geostrategic ally of the United States.

While the experiences of the Second World War provided the rationale for this project of European integration, the geographical definition of membership was more troubling. Who could join this new economic club? Where did Europe begin and end? Did member countries have to be predominantly Christian in national ethos and outlook? In 1963, Turkey, often described as a geographical bridge between Europe and Asia, first applied to join the EEC and has had a problematic relationship with existing members ever since. Forty years later, Turkey's entry into the European Union remains mired in controversy as some later members such as Austria have articulated fears that this populous country will place considerable economic, political, and cultural strains on the existing membership, and others have drawn attention to the fact that Turkey's commitment to human rights and the protection of ethnic and cultural minorities has been patchy to put it mildly. Lurking beneath debates over labour movement, economic opportunities, human rights, and political integration, critics in Turkey and beyond believe there is a fundamental cultural anxiety concerning the integration of additional Muslims into a Europe that already possesses substantial Muslim communities in France and Germany.

Historically, geographical representations of Europe have changed and it would be fallacious in the extreme to contend that there are secure understandings of this continental space. Recent debates over the future of the European Union have frequently been populated with concerns relating to territory, identity, prosperity, and sovereignty (see Box 12). In the midst of the Bosnian wars in the early 1990s, European Union states were berated for being

Box 12. Euro crisis and the PIGS

The financial crisis of 2007/8 onwards rocked the confidence of many countries and regional groupings including the European Union. From 2009/10 onwards, this crisis increasingly focused on a series of EU member states nicknamed the 'PIGS'—Portugal, Ireland, Greece, and Spain, later joined by Cyprus. Each of these countries were, in return for European Central Bank assistance over their sovereign debt levels, required to undertake substantial public sector cuts and reformation of government spending and taxation. What was interesting about these austerity packages, in terms of identity politics, was the suggestion (sometimes rather unsubtle in terms of media reporting) that these 'southern European' countries with the geographical exception of Ireland were 'basket case' economies populated with communities that did not pay tax, did not work long enough, were beholden to 'dirty money' from crime syndicates, and were generally undeserving of northern European financial support. The acronym PIGS became a way of registering displeasure at the alleged behaviour of these states and was seized upon by anti-EU parties and political leaders to articulate a wider critique against EU expansion in the 1980s and 1990s onwards. What was striking was that Ireland was included as the 'I' rather than, say, debt-ridden Italy, an original member of the European Economic Community. Unsurprisingly, the German government (and largest EU economy) was perceived in some quarters to be the most strident when it came to the implementation of austerity packages.

weak and failing to intervene in an area proximate to the membership. Bosnian and other European intellectuals poured scorn on the inability of fellow Europeans to come to the aid of a multicultural and multi-ethnic country located only two hours flying time from London and even less from Paris, Bonn, and Rome. The destruction of cities such as Mostar and Sarajevo in 1992 and the massacre of 7,000 men and boys in Srebrenica in 1995 was interpreted by many observers as a damning indictment of the failure of this European project to promote values such as integration, tolerance, peace, and democracy.

In the midst of the negotiations relating to a European Constitution, political parties and media outlets debated with some vigour the nature and purpose of the European Union, which now comprised 27 member states. Some political figures on the right wished to see the Constitution embody a 'Christian European' ethos and place due emphasis on its geographical identity as a distinct civilization. French and Dutch voters later rejected the proposed Constitution and thus effectively derailed the introduction of this particular body of text. For non-Christian observers, the notion that Europe could ever be defined as a Christian space would be alarming, given the long-standing presence of Jewish and Muslim communities throughout the continent and in prospective candidate states such as Turkey. However, it should not be assumed that these cultural-religious questions sit uneasily with secular Enlightenment ideals, as human rights and individual freedoms are attractive to all Europeans including Turks.

One of the greatest challenges facing many European governments including Britain, France, and the Netherlands is the alienation faced by Muslim communities. One of the 11 September hijackers, Mohammed Atta, was deeply disillusioned with German society while studying in Hamburg. In France, rioting in the suburbs of Paris in the summer of 2005 was blamed on the discrimination and racism faced by young Muslim men in particular. Local experiences of alienation coupled with the ongoing crises in Afghanistan, Palestine, Iraq, and Chechnya have contributed to a global sense of grievance. This combination of local, regional, and global religious and geopolitical factors was cited as significant in the motivation of the four men who chose to bomb the London transport system on 7 July 2005.

Such cultural debates over the geographical extent of Europe haunt many narratives of national identity and pan-regional expressions. Turkey's long-standing engagement with the European Union is just one aspect of this predicament, as were the wars that engulfed the former Yugoslavia in the early 1990s. Other areas of pan-European political and cultural life, such as the flow of people both inside the European Union and outside, have frequently provoked anxieties about who is European and who is not. The recent entry of Poland and Slovakia into the EU led some British newspapers to warn that Britain would be 'swamped' as Eastern Europeans migrated to Britain in search of work opportunities. As with immigration from the so-called New Commonwealth in the 1950s and 1960s, some commentators claimed that the country was on the verge of being overwhelmed by people who were not 'like us'. As with contemporary debates over immigration, references to 'swamping' act as a kind of cultural geographical code to enact worries about national and even pan-regional identities. For those with a keener sense of history and geography, countries such as Britain have always been shaped by waves of immigrants. The Polish Community in the United Kingdom is now one of the largest and numbers around 1 million.

The membership of the European Union continues to expand, with Bulgaria and Romania joining in January 2007. While many have been critical of EU institutions and its incapacity to generate an effective sense of purpose and pan-European identity, it is necessary to consider how the EU has encouraged new expressions of national identity. In May 2006, the republic of Montenegro held a referendum for independence and 55 per cent voted in favour of that option at the expense of continued partnership with Serbia. The role of the EU is particularly interesting because it established the criteria which the republic of Montenegro should meet in order to have its claims of independence acknowledged. Indeed, the key argument for Montenegrin independence was shaped by a desire to enter the EU, not national independence per se. Many Montenegrins were unhappy that their desire to be part of the EU was being effectively suspended because of Serbian unwillingness to surrender suspected war criminals and previous involvement in violent conflicts involving Kosovo and other parts of the former Yugoslavia. The participation of the EU was without precedent and clearly demonstrates how a pan-European organization can play a decisive role in shaping cultural claims to a European identity.

As with the Baltic countries, such as Estonia, Lithuania and Latvia, membership of the European Union was seen as an important part of a transformative process which would allow these states to reimagine themselves as 'European' and at the same time less bound up with the affairs and interests of the former Soviet Union. In doing so, the European Union becomes less geographically defined by Western European states and therefore more internally differentiated. But all of this has come under greater stress in more recent years as two issues—economic austerity and immigration control (Figure 8)—increasingly dominate relationships not only within the EU but also with proximate regions such as North Africa. In January 2014, Romanian and Bulgarian migrants were allowed to enter other EU labour markets such as the UK, and this provoked a great deal of commentary (once again) about whether the UK was going to be overwhelmed by another wave of East European migrants. Meanwhile, aspirant countries such as Ukraine are struggling to mitigate an internal schism regarding greater orientation towards the EU on the one hand and Russia on the other hand.

The identity narratives and political practices associated with the European Union have both complemented and challenged those

8. Vigil for those who died off Lampedusa on 7 October 2013 in Valetta, Malta. Some 300 people drowned when a boat sank carrying migrants from North Africa

associated with national states. For some the European Union should be considered as a 'Europe of nations', while others seek to encourage a 'United States of Europe'. One way of dealing with these competing geopolitical visions is simply to resolve them geographically; the Euro-zone and the Schengen Agreement provide examples where some states are members and others are not. The accompanying debates over the geographical extension of Europe are important, as the EU has shown itself willing to extend European Union activities beyond the boundaries of the current membership. In 2006, the EU approved the deployment of a contingent of over 7,000 largely European troops, led by Italy and France, to southern Lebanon. The new UNIFIL force was an unprecedented effort—both in terms of scope but also because it created a new UN–EU peace-keeping force. The EU now contributes to a variety of other humanitarian missions around the world: from the Congo to East Timor to Transdniestria/Moldova. What is more, both Lebanese and Israeli commentators have called for further European involvement in a territorial region which in the case of Israel is part of European football and singing-related contests. The EU has acknowledged Hezbollah is an important non-state organization that needs to be brought into the negotiating equation.

Geopolitics and subnational identity

If regional expressions of identity and purpose complicate the relationship between political entities and expressions of national identity, subnational groupings seeking independence or greater autonomy from a central authority also question any simple assumptions that identities are territorially bounded. Countries such as Japan and Iceland, which are virtually ethnically homogeneous have had less experience of subnational groupings challenging territorial legitimacy and associated claims to national identity. Within Europe, communities such as the Catalan community in Spain and the Walloons in Belgium continue to provide reminders that expressions of national unity and purpose are circumscribed and sometimes violently contested by other groupings that resent claims to a national identity or vision. Nation building is a dynamic process and states such as Spain have alternated between trying to repress and to accommodate competing demands for particular territorial units and representations of identity therein. Over the last 40 years, Spanish governments based in Madrid have granted further autonomy to the Catalan and Basque communities, at the same time as military officials have been quoted as noting that the country would never allow those regions to break away from Spain (Box 13).

This apparent determination to hold on to those territories has in part provoked groups such as ETA (Basque Homeland and Freedom in English) to pursue terror campaigns that have in the past included bombings and attacks on people and property in the Basque region and major cities such as Madrid. Created in July 1959, it sought to promote Basque nationalism alongside an anti-colonial message which called for the removal of Spain's

Box 13. National rivalries: football and Spain

An insight into the contested national condition is provided by football. The Spanish league (*La Liga*) provides opportunities for fans and political leaders to project their frustrations and ambitions onto the backs of rival football teams. Basque and Catalan teams (such as Athletic Bilbao and Barcelona respectively) are important expressions of regional identity and pride. Matches against Real Madrid (supported by the Spanish dictator Franco) are particularly intense and represent a very real expression of popular geopolitics, especially those involving the world-class Barcelona FC (now sponsored by Qatar Airways after a long history of refusing commercial sponsorship). Franco attempted to use Real Madrid's success in the European Cup to suppress regional and linguistic differences within Spain. The Catalan language was banned under his period of rule (1939–75).

occupation. The Spanish leader General Franco was a fierce opponent and used paramilitary groups to attempt to crush ETA. This proved unsuccessful and ETA continued to operate after his death in 1975, notwithstanding various attempts to secure a ceasefire in the 1990s. Most importantly, the group was initially blamed for the Madrid bombing on 11 March 2004, which cost the lives of nearly 200 people. Islamic militant groups rather than ETA were the perpetrators of the Madrid bombings (called '11-M' in Spain). The then People's Party government led by Prime Minister Jose Aznar, who had approved the deployment of Spanish troops to Iraq, was heavily defeated at the national election three days later. Interestingly, a national government haunted by low popularity attempted to blame an organization operating within Spain for a bombing that many believed to be a direct consequence of Spain's willingness to support the War on Terror.

While the challenge to the Spanish state posed by subregional nationalisms remains, the use of terror probably receded as a consequence of the March 2004 attacks on Madrid. As with other regional movements, found in Catalonia and Galicia, groups such as ETA play a part in mobilizing narratives of identity which run counter to national stories about Spain and Spanish identities. The separatists unsurprisingly either target property and symbols emblematic of the Spanish state and its 'colonial occupation' or vigorously promote practices and expressions of difference such as languages, regional flags, and maps and in the case of ETA a geographical space that defines and defends the Basque homeland—Euskalherria. It is, however, important to note that not all Basque separatists have supported the activities of ETA in the past.

The apparent challenge posed by subnational groupings is not unique to Europe, however. In China, for instance, the central authorities in Beijing have identified separatist movements in western China as a major security threat, especially post-9/11. Since coming to power in 1949, the Chinese Communist Party has been anxious to preserve territorial integrity in the face of the de facto secession of Taiwan and the troubling occupation of Tibet. More recently, Muslim separatists in the far west of China have been represented as a threat to Chinese unity and sense of national identity. In the last five years, the central government has adopted a fourfold strategy to promote national unity—economic investment directed towards those regions containing separatists in the hope of removing grievances over regional inequalities, population movement from East to West China, an enhanced internal security presence, and via foreign policy decisions such as the pursuing of close cooperation with Central Asian states and Russia. As others have noted, China has used America's War on Terror opportunistically to repress further any communities and groupings judged to be threatening to national security.

For both national states and regional separatists, the struggles to demarcate ownership of territory are considered to be an essential element in enabling particular narratives of identity to be sustained. On the one hand, these struggles in diverse places such as Spain, China, Sri Lanka, or Indonesia help national governments not only to legitimate military and security operations but frequently they also provoke greater levels of financial and emotional investment in narratives of national identity as manifested in popular cultural outlets such as television, schools, and newspapers. The designation of something as a security threat, as scholars of geopolitics and international relations have noted, is often an essential moment in the justification of coercive means as the state is judged to be imperilled. On the other hand, separatist struggles remind us that such claims to national identities are never given. The contemporary condition of places like Iraq, Lebanon, and Syria provides a chilling reminder of how colonial borders and multiple identities coexist uneasily and the imposition of infrastructure and national symbols such as a national flags and currencies is barely adequate when there is little local legitimacy and recognition.

Following 9/11 and the decision by the United States to declare a War on Terror, it is striking how apparent allies such as Russia, China, and others such as Israel have sought to rebrand local separatist/self-determination struggles as part of a broader global narrative of counter-terror. Often geopolitically opportunistic in the extreme, it does highlight the continued importance of geographical scale in political and cultural life. The subnational, the national, and the global are implicated with one another. President Putin, as part of this global counter-terror movement, has represented Russia's violent interventions in Chechnya, which predate 9/11, as a response to the threat facing the territorial integrity of Russia. Ironically, and in large measure because of the disproportionate levels of civilian losses, Islamic militants have seized upon the behaviour of Russian troops to justify not only terror acts in the region, such as the murderous assault on a school in Beslan in neighbouring North Ossetia in 2004, but elsewhere in Iraq and Israel. More recently, the shopping mall massacre in Nairobi in September 2013 was justified as an angry reaction to Kenyan military involvement in Somalia.

Geopolitics and civilizations

In 1993, the American scholar Samuel Huntington created something of a stir when he published an essay entitled 'The Clash of Civilizations' in the journal *Foreign Affairs*. As with Francis Fukuyama's contribution 'The End of History', a striking title and opportune timing ensured that the essay received considerable publicity both in the United States and elsewhere, including the Middle East and Islamic world. The article begins in dramatic fashion:

> World politics is entering a new phase, and intellectuals [such as himself] have not hesitated to proliferate visions of what it will be the end of history, the return of traditional rivalries between nation-states, and the decline of the nation-state from the conflicting pulls of tribalism and globalism, among others. Yet they all miss a crucial, indeed a central, aspect of what global politics is likely to be in the coming years.... The clash of civilizations will dominate global politics. The fault lines between civilizations will be the battle lines of the future.

Over the pages that follow, Huntington sets out his intellectual stall with a bold, sweeping analysis of the geographies of global politics rather reminiscent of earliest geopolitical writers commentating at the start of the 20th century.

Critically, Huntington sketches a new world map populated by seven or possibly eight civilizations, rather than one dominated by a geographical heartland. In Huntington's geopolitical world, the principal threat facing Western civilization is judged to be Islam and its associated territorial presence in the Middle East, North Africa, Central Asia, and Asia. While his understanding of civilization is vague, his depiction of Islamic civilizations as

89

threatening is informed by the published writings of the Middle Eastern and Islamic scholar Bernard Lewis. The latter has been instrumental in informing neo-conservative opinion in the United States and more than any other scholar has arguably helped to inform the intellectual framework of the George W. Bush administration with regard to foreign policy options for the Middle East. Unsurprisingly, other well known scholars such as the Palestinian-American academic Edward Said have been scathing of the work of Huntington and Lewis.

In defining Islamic civilizations as inherently threatening to the United States and the West more generally, an identity politics reminiscent of the cold war continues albeit under a different cultural-geographical guise. If communism and the Soviet Union were considered global threats for 60 years, Said and others contend that it is now the turn of Islam and regions such as the Middle East and North Africa to be depicted as dangerous and threatening. Even if such an apparent master-narrative seems simplistic, Huntington's mental mapping of the world contains some extraordinary silences or omissions. For one thing, the notion that the West is defined as Christian seems to neglect the long-term presence of other faith communities in Europe and North America. Moreover, it is difficult to imagine any civilization that has not been influenced by a whole range of flows including people and their faiths and other socio-cultural practices, including language, food, and architecture. Any visitor to Spain and Portugal would be hard pushed not to notice the continued influence of Islamic architecture and the role of Arabic in determining place names, for example.

More worryingly for Edward Said, in an article entitled 'The Clash of Ignorance' and published in October 2001, the idea of a 'clash of civilizations' informs an American world view, which might interpret the attacks of 11 September 2001 in distinctly cultural terms. While some Islamic militants might invoke such cultural terms, the inherent danger in such simplistic labelling of places is that interdependence and complexity are sacrificed in favour of monochromatic simplicities. Again, in Bush's America, there is no shortage of right-wing commentators such as Ann Coulter only too eager to link Christian/Western superiority to a form of American foreign policy which would advocate the unqualified defence of Israel and the destruction of the Islamic world. For the more extreme elements of the Christian evangelical community, the Second Coming of Christ will only be secured once the world encounters Armageddon even via a clash with Islamic militants, or more prosaically via global climate change.

Regardless of the source of global destruction, the 'clash of civilizations' debate has highlighted how narratives of identity are also articulated at a global level. These kinds of debates, however, often neglect key elements such as the historical geographies of colonialism. If one wants to understand the ways in which different places and faiths have interacted with one another then the legacies of cultural, political, and economic dominance and resistance have to be appreciated. Again the inherent danger of the Huntington thesis is that other places and faith communities are simply represented as threatening. Even if they were, it is striking that commentators such as Huntington and Lewis are unwilling to consider in more detail how the experiences of British and French colonial domination in the Middle East shaped and continues to shape contemporary geopolitical relations. Claims to British or French moral superiority were frequently exposed when those countries subsequently bombed, gassed, and massacred the very populations they sought to order and control.

Egypt in the early 1920s and 1930s was filled with foreign soldiers and social spaces were segregated in favour of Europeans in a manner later to be replicated in apartheid South Africa. A mounting sense of humiliation and iniquity in Egypt later played a key role in informing the creation of the Muslim Brotherhood and the anti-colonial campaign against the British thereafter. Egyptian radicals such as Sayyid Qutb later visited the United States in

1948 and reported his dislike of its materialistic culture and racial discrimination, especially against the African-American community. While there have been a variety of sources and contexts which have inspired contemporary Islamic militancy, the living memories of colonial occupation combined with a dislike of the racist nature of Western liberal-democratic states is part of that complex equation. Western powers, with the help of proxy regimes such as Egypt, Saudi Arabia, and Jordan, continued to interfere in the affairs of these states even when they had obtained formal independence. Iranians to this day still highlight the role of the American Central Intelligence Agency in sponsoring a coup against the reforming Mossadegh government in 1953.

The 'clash of civilizations' promises cultural and geographical simplicities, which frankly don't square with the complexities of a world filled with interconnected communities and diasporic networks including Christians, Druze, and many Arabic-speaking Muslim communities (Figure 9). Such simplicities might make for comforting reading/listening in some parts of the world but are insufficiently attentive to the complexities of human mobility and accompanying demands that communities might and do make on an array of governments and organizations. Given recent concern over the state of Syria, in the midst of widespread conflict, it is sobering to think that there might be around 18 million people living outside Syria who have Syrian heritage including well-known US personalities such as Teri Hatcher and the late Apple boss, Steve Jobs.

Against this geopolitical backdrop, the late Osama bin Laden and his associates presented their struggle as one directed against 'Jews and Crusaders' operating in the Middle East and elsewhere. In his publicized speeches, bin Laden utilized the 'clash of civilizations' to help explain and legitimate the campaign against the United States and its allies including the apostate regimes of Egypt, Jordan, and Saudi Arabia. His desire to create a new Islamic community (umma) was based on the cultural-religious

9. Lebanese Armenians protest outside the Turkish Embassy in Rabieh, north-east Beirut, 24 April 2012 to commemorate the 97th anniversary of the Ottoman Turkish genocide against the Armenian people

purification of the Middle East and Islamic world. The ejection of Israelis, apostates, and American forces from the region is judged to be critical in achieving this objective. The latter is most clearly articulated in his 'Declaration of a Jihad against the America's occupying the land of the two holy places' and reiterated again in the aftermath of the 11 September 2001 attacks on New York and Washington. It is also perhaps not surprising that the two most formative influences on bin Laden's intellectual world view were the Palestinian Abdullah Azzam and the brother of the Egyptian activist and founder of the Muslim Brotherhood, Sayyid Qutb.

As the political geographer John Agnew has recorded by way of a concluding summary on the geopolitical imagination of bin Laden and the Al-Qaeda network:

The United States is a geopolitical abstraction seen as an earthly Satan. The religious inspiration is fundamental to its [i.e.

Al-Qaeda's] goals and to its language. These are a mirror image of the idea of the 'clash of civilizations' proposed by the American political scientist Samuel Huntington in 1993...In this case an Islamic world is seen as in a death struggle with an infidel civilization represented by the United States, captain of the materialist West....Only by expelling the West can the pollution be swept away.

Conclusions

This chapter has been concerned with the role of identity politics in shaping geopolitical relationships. This concern for narratives of identity has been provoked by a desire to further shift our interest in geopolitics away from fixed geographical conditions and the activities of great powers such as the contemporary United States and China. Recent scholarship has focused attention on how a state's relative location is constructed and what strategic meaning is given to its territory. This implies that territory is not inherently strategic, rather it has to be invested with significance. Geopolitical reasoning plays a critical role in assigning values to some communities and territories often at the expense of others. These kinds of activities become all the more poignant when a country is seeking some form of territorial redress or is presumed to be facing some kind of threat from other state and non-state organizations. Within contemporary countries and regions such as Israel/Palestine, Argentina/Chile, and Pakistan/India, there is no shortage of evidence of how forms of geopolitical reasoning are used to secure particular claims to territory and identity. This in turn leads to the frequent justification of military force (either actual or threatened), accompanied by politico-military doctrines of pre-emption and unilateral action. These claims are not only produced within government circles but are frequently reproduced within popular cultural arenas such as newspapers, magazines, and cartoons.

In other cases, comparatively new states such as Estonia and non-state organizations continue to project their own identity narratives. In the case of Estonia, membership of the European Union and the North Atlantic Treaty Organization were significant in re-orientating the country away from its association with the Soviet Union and the Eastern bloc more generally. For supporters of this geopolitical transformation, Estonia's cultural future is believed to belong to Europe, which is frequently contrasted unfavourably with non-European Russia. The European Union is conceived of both as an opportunity for Estonia to strengthen its European credentials and also as a safeguard against possible Russian interference. As with West Germany in the 1950s, integration is perceived to be strengthening rather than weakening national sovereignty. The Russian-speaking minority in Estonia are perhaps more cautious about this transformation. Paradoxically, it is 'Europe' that has come to the 'salvation' of that Russian minority (just as it would for minorities in Turkey for instance) because it is axiomatic of European Union membership that laws excluding citizens are either repealed or softened so that minority rights are recognized and protected by both national and European law.

More broadly, this discussion further reiterates the fundamental importance of territory and geographical relationships within global geopolitics. On the one hand, state territories remain terrifically important in defining national identities and it would be a complete exaggeration to claim that globalization has eroded this connection. On the other hand, the state and associated national territory coexist with a host of other geographical connections, which might be described as subnational or regional, let alone at the level of civilization. As a consequence of these permutations, individuals and communities are far more likely to lay claim to multiple identities that cross over national boundaries and identities.

Chapter 5
Geopolitics and objects

Introduction

This chapter explores the role of objects, and what the anthropologist Daniel Miller might term, stuff. Previously, in the first edition of this book, my attention was on maps as one particular form of representation but also as object—as much as paper documents as visual representations on a computer screen, or in the form of other sorts of objects such as atlases and globes let alone as applications to be downloaded on to smart phones. The focus on objects is designed to highlight that geopolitical imaginations and practices are embedded and emboldened by their relationship to a vast array of things ranging from the flag, the pipeline, the map, the gun, and as noted in this chapter even toys such as Action Man dolls and model airplanes and buildings. The examples here are not, in any sense, exhaustive. But they do point to the central importance of objects and stuff in the making of geopolitics, in all its diversity.

If we take the example, by way of exemplification, of the closed circuit television camera (CCTV) then we can begin to sketch here an object-centred agenda. One of the most extraordinary features of British (and some other national jurisdictions) urban life is the widespread presence of CCTV. In the City of London, for example, it is difficult to imagine walking down any street that does not have some kind of camera-based surveillance. It is not uncommon for police and private security officers to interrogate any passerby taking photographs of buildings and streets. Intensified in the aftermath of a terrorist attack by the IRA in 1992, the War on Terror encouraged further investment in such surveillance objects, technologies, and practices, especially following the 7 July 2005 attacks on London's transport system itself that left over 50 dead. What was interesting about this intensification process was how the CCTV unit itself (the camera) and associated networks of technology and surveillance became part and parcel of the British urban landscape. As an object it became important all the more so because there was barely any public response to its proliferation. As with those unremarked flags that Michel Billig noted in his exposition on banal nationalism, we have here a case study of how an object can become powerful precisely because it was transformed into something unremarkable, and indeed simply necessary in extraordinary times.

The role of the object in geopolitics is not always dramatic, therefore. Sometimes objects can be banal rather than 'hot' (Figure 10). Sometimes they can be militarized and sometimes mundane. The unremarked flag hanging outside a public building can be part of the taken for granted and then suddenly ripped down and burnt by angry crowds protesting about the foreign policy behaviour of a particular state. Objects can shape geopolitical relations (the protestors burning the flag are drawn into temporary and sometimes permanent alliances), and yet they can also highlight (and obscure depending on the context) state authority. So the CCTV camera is a powerful, yet largely visible, expression of state security while at the same time one which is barely challenged within everyday life by citizens. So much of contemporary life is informed by a geopolitical imaginary warning of possible terrorist attacks and emergencies, and objects play a key role in securitizing, regularizing, and disciplining our lives as we are urged to report suspicious objects, undergo screening, and accept covert and overt surveillance. While we may choose to

10. Material geopolitics? Airfix Afghan single-storey building. This model is part of a range of Afghanistan-themed models that can be assembled with a special focus on UK–US military engagements

ignore such things, objects have a way of slipping in and out of our attention spans. Whether we choose to ignore them, play with them, accept them, and/or break them, they help to bring the human and non-human elements of geopolitics into contact with one another—without assuming that objects do not enjoy their own agency to enable, disable, transform, and so on human practices (Box 14).

> ### Box 14. Secretary of State Colin Powell, PowerPoint, and Picasso's *Guernica*
>
> In February 2003, Secretary of State Colin Powell went to the United Nations Security Council to deliver a PowerPoint presentation on the WMD (weapons of mass destruction) capabilities of Iraq. Sensing that the international community was not supportive of a potential invasion of Saddam Hussein's Iraq, on the basis of either alleged complicity with the 11 September 2001 attacks and/or threatening WMD capabilities, Powell's presentation was designed to persuade and enroll support for the US case.

At the same time as Powell was using Microsoft PowerPoint to unveil objects such as biological weapons facilities, another object (a tapestry) was being veiled. Prior to his presentation, UN information officers were asked to cover up Picasso's famous depiction of the Nazi aerial bombardment of the Spanish village of Guernica. Created in 1937, the painting depicted the horrific consequences of bombing on a civilian population and a tapestry reproduction was donated to the United Nations by the Nelson Rockefeller Foundation in 1985. It has, since that time, hung outside the entrance to the UN Security Council. The tapestry was completely covered up for the duration of Powell's presentation presumably because it was felt that the object itself was a powerful counterpoint to what was being called for, namely the assault on the country and population of Iraq. Anti-war protestors seized on that request and highlighted how the United States was attempting to visually manage the build-up to the invasion of Iraq in March 2003. But it also reminds us how objects themselves, and not just what they depict in the case of *Guernica*, have tremendous vibrancy. The full-size tapestry itself is a substantial object in its own right and since 2009 no longer hangs outside the UN Security Council. It is now on loan to a US-based art gallery.

Pipelines

Let us start with an object, or series of objects, that are often held to be emblematic of energy security and resource geopolitics: the pipeline. As an object, albeit a highly complex one, involving pump stations, feeder pipelines, and terminals, it has been enormously productive of geopolitics. The Trans-Alaska Pipeline (TAP), built in the mid-1970s, is one of the longest pipeline systems in the world stretching from Prudhoe Bay in the north of the state of Alaska to the port of Valdez in the south (Figure 11). Built in the aftermath of the 1973 oil crisis, it was intended as a dramatic response to anxieties that American energy security was

11. Pipeline geopolitics: the Trans-Alaska Pipeline

increasingly beholden to a small group of oil-producing exporting
countries in the Middle East and elsewhere such as Nigeria and
Venezuela. The sharp rise in oil price transformed the discovered
and undiscovered potential of the Prudhoe Bay oil field, where
petroleum resources had been found in the late 1960s.

The construction of the pipeline was hugely challenging, as the
immense metal structure needed to be able to withstand extreme
weather and hundreds of miles of challenging and changeable
Arctic landscapes. The flow of oil began in 1977 and since the late
1970s the TAP has facilitated the shipping of over 15 billion
barrels of oil. The production and circulation of oil transformed
the Alaskan economy and the parameters of the US energy
security debates. But it was also deeply controversial and divisive.
So while the TAP was a response to global energy shifts, the
pipeline itself as an object was a source of discord. For
conservationists, the TAP was emblematic of a 'rush to oil'
regardless of the cumulative impact of a large construction
project, which was operating in an environment subject to

climatic extremes. For native populations, the pipeline project appeared to be not only indifferent to the consequences of placing a large object over vast sways of the Alaskan landscape but also inattentive to revenue sharing. Who would benefit from the flow of oil from northern Alaska to the south, and would it be only the 'Lower 48'? In October 1971, President Nixon agreed to the Alaska Native Claims Settlement Act, which stipulated that if native Alaskans renounced their land claims in the areas affected by the pipeline project then the US government would transfer $900 million and 148 million acres of federal land in compensation. The provisions of the Settlement Act were distributed amongst the communities concerned and, as a consequence, the TAP project was completed.

The TAP pipeline was not only productive of global energy geopolitics but also indigenous geopolitics, which brought to the fore how indigenous communities were treated by federal/state-level governments. Since its entry into the union in 1959, the state of Alaska was depicted as both a resource frontier but also a highly militarized space, at the frontline in terms of cold war antagonism with the Soviet Union. Less concern, however, was expressed for indigenous and northern communities, who were more likely to be considered 'obstacles' to security and development. The pipeline, in its various manifestations, transformed the geopolitics of Alaska and altered profoundly the manner in which this territory and its infrastructure was imagined and managed.

But the pipeline system, as a complex object, can also produce different kinds of geopolitical relations. In the winter of 2006–7, European media outlets were releasing multiple stories about Russian gas supplies and the role of Ukraine as a pivotal state lying betwixt Russia as supplier and Western Europe as market. The disruption of supply, prompted by an argument between Ukraine and Russia over gas prices and lack of payment on the part of Ukraine, led to speculation that gas supplies would be disrupted and Western European homes would be starved of heating. Russia accused Ukraine of 'stealing' $25 million of gas exports destined for European customers and other countries such as Moldava complained of being 'cut off' because they failed to pay the price charged by the Russian supplier, Gazprom. Maps of European gas pipelines further reinforced the geopolitical power of the pipeline itself and in particular the capacity of Russian gas producers to alter or even stop the flow of gas. The mobility of gas, as enabled by the pipeline, appeared in peril. Transit countries, such as Ukraine and Belarus, were re-imagined as strategically significant precisely because supplies of gas had to pass through pipeline infrastructure located within their national territories. For some commentators, the 'gas war' was indicative of a resurgent Russia, eager to remind the world that it was an 'energy superpower' with the pipeline enrolled as 'evidence' of such a proposition. Without gas, the pipeline's promise of regular supply to European markets was dashed.

Objects such as pipelines can, as a consequence, inspire fear, hope, intrigue, and even dread. In the James Bond adventure, *The World is not Enough* (1999), the British secret agent is sent to Azerbaijan to investigate a possible plot to disrupt a transnational pipeline project. European energy security appears to be at stake and Bond eventually uncovers a plot not only to disrupt the pipeline but also to launch a nuclear assault of the Turkish city of Istanbul in order to disrupt tanker traffic via the Black Sea. Standing by a computer-generated map of the Caspian Sea region, Electra King explains to Bond that there are a series of rival projects and that her sponsored project faces industrial sabotage. As explained in the next section, the map as object is critical in the film and on several occasions its existence is used to account for the apparent geopolitical stakes. Maps, pipelines, tankers, nuclear bombs, and submarines play a critical role in shaping this resource-based drama. The inference being that the energy security of states is a complex game where states, including the UK, need to be ever vigilant for either disruption or commercial advantage. The pipeline is fizzing with possibilities—if secured it promises to transform state power but if disrupted then the consequences might be dire.

Maps

At times of war and international discord, it is perhaps not surprising that public interest in maps and the places they represent is greatest. The power of the map lies not just in its ability to represent places and peoples in multiple ways and be understood in a variety of ways as well. As Benedict Anderson noted, the map (and manifestations such as the British imperial map which depicted colonies and territories as either red or pink in colour) was instrumental in shaping generations of citizens, and how they divided the world up into distinct places and zones. In the cold war period, the development of the North Pole-centred azimuthal projections were credited with introducing American citizens to a new way of looking at the world, one in which the relative geographical proximity of the Soviet Union, via the Arctic, was emphasized. More generally, such projections were credited with shaping a new 'air-age', where the flight path of the plane reshaped a sense of distance and geographical relationship with other countries and continents.

As an object, it can be pointed at, torn up, altered, hidden, and generally put to work in cementing state power. As documents, therefore, maps play an important role in the making of geopolitics, which exceeds their practical value in terms of locating places and helping users navigate more generally. The map has been central to the mediation of states and the international system, especially when it comes to the delimitation of international borders. Other objects such as stones, trees, signposts, and barbed wire were essential elements in the articulation of borders, as well as features such as rivers and mountain ranges. With the development of scientific cartography from the 16th century onwards, the production of maps was increasingly significant in outlining the boundaries of states and their existence helped to facilitate subsequent endeavours to mark and secure borders. This process continues apace in the maritime domain with coastal states investing large sums of money to map and chart their outer continental shelves in the expectation that sovereign authority can be extended over the seabed (with the promise of greater access to resources lying on or below the ocean floor).

The map can also be tremendously productive of contemporary geopolitics. A striking example is the recent publication of a national map by China. Produced by Sino Maps Press, a cartographic body under the control of the State Bureau of Surveying and Mapping, the map was released in September 2013. What was notable about it was the capacity of its existence to generate unease among neighbouring South-East Asian states. The unease was in part representational but also rooted in an appreciation that the map as object is intimately linked to manifestations of state power. In many countries, and China is not unique in this regard, the production of national maps depicting territorial extent and boundaries is officially controlled. There are official producers and suppliers of maps. Such national maps may also be reproduced on other objects such as passports (as is the case in Argentina and China). What caused most concern in the case of the Chinese national map was the depiction of the South China Sea. As some analysts noted, the latest iteration introduced a so-called 10th dash on to the map itself implying that China enjoyed strategic interest across this maritime region, extending now to the north. The addition of the 10th dash now enrolled Taiwan into this strategic perimeter.

The South China Sea is a deeply contested maritime region. A number of islands are disputed and as a consequence so too are claims to maritime authority in the form of territorial seas, exclusive economic zones, and even sovereign rights to the extended continental shelf. China is locked into a conflict involving the Philippines, Vietnam, Brunei, Indonesia, and Malaysia as well as a long-standing dispute with Japan over the islands of Senkaku/Diaoyu further north. Within the legend itself, the map caused alarm because the dash is similar to uncontested national boundaries regarding land borders. In other words, the appearance of the dash would seem to suggest that China considers its sovereign authority to extend virtually all over the South China Sea. While the map acknowledges the 'boundary not defined', this map has become, quite literally, an object of discord. The ambiguity of the 'dash' on the map contributes, it is argued, to regional anxieties about the present and indeed future intent of China and its projection of maritime sovereignty.

Finally, the map as an object can become an object of counter-geopolitics. So far we have talked about fairly conventional maps and map making, as tied to the state and its geographical imagination. The experimental geographer Trevor Paglen has been a notable example using new cartographic technologies and applications (e.g. Google Earth) and visual methodologies to generate different kinds of mappings. Since the onset of the War on Terror in 2001, Paglen has revealed other invisible objects too such as CIA extraordinary rendition flights and an accompanying network of destinations and stop off points including Jordan, Ireland, Qatar, Libya, Afghanistan, and Guantánamo Bay (Cuba). Working with artists and curators, his publications, including *An Atlas of Radical Cartography*, considers a number of maps including images of US oil consumption, and European Union detention patterns regarding illegal migrants. The term radical cartography, or indeed counter-cartography, is intended therefore to do two things: first, to highlight what conventional maps (often preoccupied with state territories and international/domestic boundaries/jurisdictions) simply miss or under-emphasize; second, to challenge, politically and geographically speaking, as a consequence, phenomena and relationships that might not be considered worthy of being mapped. So while we can imagine why US government authorities might have been reluctant to produce official maps showing the flight paths of extraordinary rendition-related planes, we might also wonder why other maps are never drawn in the first place. When North American and European governments express anxiety about illegal migration, we might juxtapose the actual numbers of such migrants with the kinds of figures having to be handled by other states like Pakistan and Jordan in the aftermath of civil war, disaster, and the like. Such maps may make use of data sources that are ignored or marginalized in mainstream geopolitical debate.

As maps are increasingly thought of as being the products of geographical information systems rather than hand drawn by a coterie of skilled artists/technicians so the map as a digital tool is potentially more widely available than ever before. Artists, as well as citizens more generally, are developing their own maps and these virtual objects are interacting with the material world. Maps, however, continue to be powerful precisely because they can highlight some things at the expense of others and the work of Paglen and others is about challenging the notion that the map is an object or manifestation of state power. So what is significant is not just the representational qualities of the digital map (in other words, the actual content) but also that it mimics the material qualities of official maps—with legends, scale, and so on.

The flag

When crowds gather outside embassies and diplomatic missions and burn the national flag of the country concerned, you can assume reasonably that there is something rather powerful about the flag itself. Angry protestors in Argentina, for example, have routinely burned the British flag as a way of registering their anger against continued occupation of the Falkland Islands (Islas Malvinas). The American and Israeli flags are often burnt in the Middle East and Islamic world as a protest against US and Israeli security policies (including the use of drones in places like Pakistan) and the continued Israeli occupation of the West Bank.

The Danish flag was burnt in the aftermath of the controversy regarding a series of published cartoons in a regional Danish newspaper that were said to insult the Prophet Mohammed. So the flag as an object of geopolitical hate is significant. It would not be unreasonable to assume that some national flags are far more likely to get burnt (e.g. the US, the UK, and Israeli flags) than others (e.g. Belgium, Sweden, and Bhutan).

The flag as an object is also a powerful accomplice to nation-state formation and national identity politics. Theorists such as Émile Durkheim, who noted the material and symbolic qualities of flags, recognized these properties. Flags may well be powerful signifiers of nations, values, and geographical spaces but their very materiality is also significant. Flags are defended in their own right and the desecration of the flag is considered to be hugely provocative. In August 2013, a US rock band, Bloodhound Gang, briefly enjoyed widespread headlines for a stunt involving a band member stuffing the Russian flag into his trousers and then throwing it back into the crowd while performing in the Ukraine. The incident was caught on video and, after mass circulation, the Russian authorities condemned the incident and the band was caught up in a scuffle with protestors when they were at a Russian airport.

At times of formal ceremonies, the hoisting of national and regional flags is tremendously significant (Box 15). One example that was very striking to this author was in Nuuk (Greenland) on 21 June 2012—Greenland's national day. Gathering in the old part of Nuuk, which still bares the architectural and place-naming legacies of Danish colonial settlement and incorporation, crowds were waving both the Danish and Greenlandic flags. A formal ceremony followed, involving speeches delivered in both languages, and further formality with large flags being hoisted. Stirring brass band music accompanied some of the ceremony itself. What was deeply affecting was witnessing the assembled crowds waving both flags in a prevailing geopolitical context of autonomy and discussions

Box 15. Redesigning the flag: Australia

The Australian (and for that matter the New Zealand) flag is distinctive for its Blue Ensign located in the top left corner of the flag. Notwithstanding the presence of the Commonwealth star and the five stars of the Southern Cross, it was designed to commemorate the establishment of the Australian Federation in 1901. The 3rd of September was declared as Australia National Flag Day, and the flag's design changed slightly over the decades until being formally recognized in the 1953 Flags Act. The Act itself stipulates a series of regulations in terms of when and how the flag must be flown and insists that degraded flags must not be used. There is even guidance as to how the decayed or faded flag should be disposed of—cut up into small pieces and disposed of sensitively. The flag is not only a symbol of Australia. It is a material object and one that, as the 1953 Flags Act suggests, should be treated with decorum. But the current flag is also controversial, being considered to be indicative of a 'white and colonial' Australia, which betrays the close constitutional connection to the formal imperial power, the United Kingdom, and its interests, such as military service. Until 1953, the Australian flag was in effect the Union Jack. Some are now calling for a new flag which better represents the multi-cultural and multi-ethnic character of the country.

about future independence. Other objects such as oil, gas, rubies, and uranium have become deeply politicized as the community of 56,000 discusses and engages with resource-related futures. After the ceremony itself, the crowd retired to the town hall to enjoy an impromptu breakfast surrounded by flags and other paraphernalia associated with the national day. It was difficult not to wonder when there might be a national day where the Danish flag did not feature at all. So perhaps here the flag might be thought of as both an object of hope but also, for some, a warning of what might follow if independence from Denmark is secured.

For one thing, the large block grant given by Copenhagen to the Greenlandic government in Nuuk would cease.

The flag might also be an object capable of being enrolled in counter-geopolitics. Just as the map might be put to work in dissenting contexts, the flag is a striking accomplice to such politics. One example would be the Idle No More movement in Canada. Created in December 2012, it remains a lively protest movement involving aboriginal communities protesting against the perceived abuses of indigenous treaty rights by the conservative government in Ottawa led by Stephen Harper. One of the most noticeable flags, originating from the movement, has been to juxtapose native Indian figures and symbols onto the Canadian national flag to register protest and dissent on the very material representation of Canadian national identity. At the heart of the protests lies an assertion that the Canadian federal government is intent on diminishing indigenous sovereignty and treaty rights in the name of energy and development projects. As with other parts of the world, the pipeline is a key element in this resistance movement as well, with complaints mounting that energy projects in places like Alberta and Northwest Territories will be approved and intensified with little consideration given to the fate of ecosystems, landscapes, and communities directly affected by such decision making. Flags, in particular, become a highly material intervention in this discussion as they get mobilized to highlight not only the existing relationship with indigenous groups and the federal government but also to draw attention to international markets and relationships. Organizers attached to the Idle No More movement allege that Canada's desire to be considered an energy superpower is being championed at the expense of relationships within Canada's indigenous and northern communities.

The final element we might touch upon with regard to the flag, as a material object, is legacies. Flags have been planted and deposited in an extraordinary range of environments. They have been planted on top of mountains, deposited on the seabed, and left on the surface of the moon. When US astronauts deposited the US flag on the moon, for instance, an ambiguity of sorts was created—was the flag intended to remind the world that the United States was the first to reach the moon (Figure 12)? Was the flag a statement of intent that the United States might claim the moon as its own territory in due course? Was the flag intended to be representative of broader humanity? Likewise, the depositing of a Russian flag on the bottom of the central Arctic Ocean in August 2007 provoked a flurry of headlines detailing concerns that the flag was an indicator of future intentions. Russia, it was supposed, was literally bedding its sovereign interests and was determined, in due course, to exercise sovereign rights over vast

12. American flag planted on the moon. Six flags were planted on the moon and according to scientists only one flag might still be standing

sways of the Arctic Ocean seabed. While such fears were overstated, the vibrancy of images of a Russian flag attached to a titanium flagpole was extraordinary in unleashing a multitude of headlines warning of Russian geopolitical expansionism.

Trash

What might trash tell us about geopolitics? For those working on the borderlands of the United States and Mexico, material objects such as water bottles, shoes, medicines, and identity documents help to create an intimate introduction to the desperation of those who seek to cross semi-arid environments in a desperate attempt to enter the United States. For a number of writers including geographers and political scientists, the trash itself becomes a way of thinking about how the environmental circumstances surrounding the borderlands are integral to understanding border protection and regulation. Since the mid-1990s, there was a deliberate strategy on the part of the US government to shift illegal border traffic to more inaccessible and hostile parts of the border, in particular where mountains and deserts predominated. As a consequence of these 'natural barriers', the pathways of illegal migrants are more likely to involve traversing wildlife refuges and national parks which has had implications not only for the survivability of migrants but also for the impact of migration on ecosystems. For those who work on and study the borderlands, there is a greater array of objects and materials to be found either discarded or simply lost by those seeking to cross over. On the one hand, the presence of the trash has encouraged citizen groups to arrange cleaning up operations; on the other hand, human rights activists have pointed to the presence of discarded water bottles to make the case that ever-greater numbers of migrants are perishing due to dehydration in these unforgiving semi-arid environments pointing to what they argue is the outcome of those very border security strategies, which were designed to deter (or worse encourage a higher human toll by the strengthening of border infrastructure closer to well-known border crossing points).

So these objects become a way of documenting and recording the by-products of illegal migration and border security practices.

But waste can intervene in other ways and be productive of geopolitics. What might the dumping of waste tell us about how places and communities are inserted into circuits of power? One notorious example involves the Dutch company Trafigura, which was accused of offloading some highly toxic waste in the African country of Ivory Coast in 2006. A local dumping company was subsequently accused of illegally disposing of the waste rather than processing it safely. The controversy intensified as reports unfolded of death and illness being attributable to the illegal dumping. Trafigura was forced to pay compensation to the Ivory Coast government. What transformed this case into something more notorious was a long-drawn-out legal conflict involving attempts to impose a super-injunction preventing news media organizations reporting on the toxic waste dumping and contesting claims that the incident revealed corporate malfeasance and human rights abuses. What provided a further element of controversy was the geography of disposal. The opportunistic choice of a West African state raised the spectre that this was a deliberate attempt to ensure that European populations were not directly affected, and a cynical strategy to avoid higher waste processing costs in a country such as the Netherlands. In November 2012, the company agreed a settlement with the Dutch authorities entailing a fine and compensation package.

The geopolitics of waste is often indicative of a transnational, multi-dimensional, and uneven activity involving production, transportation, disposal, and recycling. As the Trafigura scandal demonstrated, multiple actors were involved including companies, communities, governments, media, and non-governmental organizations. But sometimes 'waste' and 'trash' can offer opportunities as well. One only has to think of examples when cargo, often in the form of containers, falls away (by accident or design) from ships, planes, and trucks and ends up in accessible areas such as beaches, encouraging local communities to take opportunities to 'recover' objects from those containers. Accidental waste, in the case of the shipping accident, becomes an opportunity for others to benefit from such flotsam and jetsam.

Waste geopolitics is not just an earthly matter either. While there are atmospheric wastes, such as pollutants held responsible for thinning the ozone layer, there is also space debris. In the mid-1990s, an intergovernmental space debris coordination committee was established involving the major players (e.g. Europe, United States, China, India, Japan, and Russia) but the recommendations of the committee are voluntary. Space trash had raised the possibility of space collision and there is growing investment in space surveillance programmes in order to enhance national capabilities to monitor and track debris movements. Collisions do occur, however, and in February 2009 a pair of Russian and US satellites hit one another. Due to the extreme sensitivity of their satellite operations, the two countries do not share or coordinate data. EU attempts to promote a Code of Conduct for Outer Space Activities (promoted since 2010) remains mired in disagreement. While most parties accept that space debris is an issue, there is a concern that China, Russia, and the United States appear unable to agree on how to address the problem of space trash and whether any measures designed to mitigate should be binding. This might change, of course, if the debris proves more disruptive of existing satellite operations. Further collisions might then hasten interest in implementing a more binding agreement on space debris.

Action toys

Recent work in critical geopolitics has addressed a field called 'ludic geopolitics', with due emphasis given to toys and connections to playful practices. Toys have had a long-standing relationship to militarism and warfare. They have been, and continue to be, used in recruitment drives, equipment design and testing, and as objects designed to legitimate and justify military behaviour. In the cold war era, rocket and tank toys made by toy manufacturers such as Dinky were designed to inculcate the young citizen with a scaled-down version of those weapon systems which were located in various locations over the globe. As children's play scholars showed, military-themed toys helped to render understandable weapons of mass destruction to a generation of children growing up at the height of the cold war, including the 'space race'.

For my generation, born in the mid to late 1960s, the introduction of the action figure looms large, especially for young boys (but not exclusively). In the United States, Hasbro launched 'GI Joe' in 1964 and within two years the UK toy manufacturer Palitoy introduced the 'Action Man'. In both cases, this toy soldier was radically different from earlier iterations of the metal figure. Designed as a mannequin doll, it was, as Tara Woodyer's research suggests, a risky business venture. Previously such dolls were associated with girls and their play-based behaviour, especially Mattel's hugely popular 'Barbie' doll. The GI Joe range was marketed as 'action' figures in order to distinguish them from the more 'passive' Barbie dolls. The design of the 'action man' was deliberate in the sense of being highly flexible and capable of being dressed and equipped in multiple iterations. For a young boy, growing up in Britain in the 1970s, my Action Man came with fuzzy hair and scarred facial skin and was equipped with hands that were able to grip a growing arsenal of weapons and assorted equipment. With a choice of clothing and vehicles, my brother and I were able to invent ever more elaborate warfare and adventure scenarios in our bedrooms (in winter) and in the garden (in the summer). Our Action Man dolls survive to this day albeit stored away in the attic of my house. What is striking, looking back at that period, is how the enemy forces were imagined to be more reminiscent of German forces in the 1940s rather than Soviet/Warsaw Pact adversaries armed with their distinctive AK-47 weapons (Box 16).

What is interesting about the development of the Action Man figures is that its design and consumer popularity enjoyed a changeable history. In the British context, Action Man was deeply nationalized, racialized, and gendered. There was no 'Action Woman' and the equipment and uniforms were based on the UK Armed Forces. There was no Black and/or Asian Action Man. All my Action Man figures were white. Members of the British military were invited by the toy manufacturers to advise on design of the dolls, and there were important variations within Western Europe. The German equivalent, during the cold war years, was less overtly militarized and equivalent figures were dressed in UN peacekeeping materials. In the United States, GI Joe became less popular in the midst of the Vietnam conflict and it was not until the emergence of Ronald Reagan as president in the 1980s that the brand was relaunched as a 'Real American Hero'.

The ebb and flow of cold war geopolitical tension plays a part in the emergence and circulation of these particular toys. But it does not explain everything. The Action Man brand was relaunched and rebranded in 1993–4 but more as an action adventure figure than a military doll. Unlike for children of my generation, the uniforms and equipment were not so rooted in recent conflict. Dressed in orange kit, the Action Man was a far cry from those earlier iterations. Action Man returned to military roots in the midst of the Victory in Europe (VE) Day commemorations in 2009. Licensed by the Ministry of Defence in the UK, the HM Armed Forces range involves the active cooperation and engagement of military personnel in the design and promotion of war toys. The marketing for these toys stresses a high level of realism in terms of clothing and equipment design. It has been actively promoted in children's magazines and via television adverts, in the midst of widespread coverage of UK military operations in Afghanistan and Iraq between 2001 and 2015.

The commercial popularity of the HM Armed Forces range is partly due to the design quality of the dolls (as noted by multiple reviewers on internet forums) but also indicative of what might be thought of as a re-enchantment with the British military forces. While not shared by all UK citizens, there has been an upsurge of 'support the troops' initiatives, including homecoming parades, 'Help the Heroes' charitable giving, commemorative ceremonies, and other activities including popular music events designed to highlight the contribution made by UK military personnel in Afghanistan in particular. Play with toys such as the HM Armed

Forces action figures becomes all the more interesting in its contribution, among many other objects such as arm bands, in domesticating and normalizing military activities and militarism more generally. But these toys can also become objects of protest and dissent, so it is important to note that the relationship between toys, militarism, and geopolitical cultures is never straightforward.

Conclusion

This new chapter on objects and material culture more generally is a recognition that geopolitics is fundamentally about stuff. The examples listed here are just that—examples and accompanying vignettes. Objects reside within networks of objects that people use, manipulate, contemplate, and so on but they are also capable of encouraging, frustrating, and even resisting human agency. The flag does tear, the gun does jam, the licensing device does fail to record, the Action Man does fall apart from childish abuse, and the container gets used to transport prisoners in Afghanistan rather than trade goods around the world.

Let me end on a salutary note. What about when the human body is objectified? In other words, what about the human beings that are sold, trafficked, and disposed of as if they were inanimate objects? Human trafficking is a multi-billion dollar industry, spanning the globe, which utilizes well-established smuggling routes and transit spaces such as Greece and Turkey in the case of movement from Asia into Western Europe. These movements are highly differentiated depending on gender, race, and age, and relationships to criminal cartels. In the most extreme examples, there are cases of sex trafficking and slavery where humans, often women, are bought and sold. In Moldova, sometimes described as the poorest country in Europe, it is estimated that around 10 per cent of the female population has been sold into prostitution, and that trafficking is rife with women heading westwards to other European countries, including the

UK. So while we may wonder about the fate of would-be migrants on flimsy boats in the southern Mediterranean, there are countless other people, often women and young girls, being objectified and transported around other parts of Europe. That is another kind of geopolitics.

Chapter 6
Popular geopolitics

For much of the last decade or so, there has been considerable interest in the popular dimensions of geopolitics and international politics. The onset of the War on Terror in October 2001 contributed to that shift, especially as news broke that the administration headed by President George W. Bush was in contact with representatives from Hollywood studios. While the relationship between US governments and the entertainment industry is well established, critics contended that this was indicative of how popular culture would inform and popularize the US-led assault on terror organizations and states judged to be supportive of terrorism (Figure 13). Such suspicions were confirmed when President Bush famously announced in May 2003 that US combat operations were complete in Iraq while standing on an aircraft carrier mimicking the generic conventions of the techno-thriller, and specifically a classic Reagan-era film, *Top Gun* (1985). Having allegedly flown a naval aircraft onto the deck of the aircraft carrier, Bush emerged in flying suit to dramatically present himself as a commander-in-chief, and after changing into a sombre suit and tie he announced in a more statesmanlike manner that hostilities were formally ending.

As became widely known, the aircraft carrier was actually stationed in the Pacific Ocean at the time but the intent was to use the generic conventions of the techno-thriller to create a particular

13. American comedian Stephen Colbert at the White House Correspondents' Dinner, 29 April 2006. Colbert was the featured entertainer at the dinner and his 16-minute performance became an internet sensation for its personal and political critique of President George W. Bush

visual aesthetic involving hyper-masculine agents, force projection, technological sophistication, and a determination to prevail against enemies. While ridiculed at the time by his critics, the 'event' itself highlighted the role of creativity and visual practices associated with movie making that was judged now to be informing political interest in reassuring the US public that the War on Terror was being won. As a type of film genre, the techno-thriller such as *Top Gun* was seen by film critics to be a popular geopolitical response to anxieties regarding earlier American 'failures' in Vietnam in the 1960s and 1970s. In the film itself, the key character Maverick is haunted by the memories of his father, a fighter pilot, who fought in the Vietnam conflict. This time, unlike Vietnam, US forces would prevail against enemy forces.

Bush's 'Top Gun' is just one example of how the geopolitical manifests itself within a popular cultural realm. Rather than just being representative of the 'real' business of geopolitics, it is more productive to think of this relationship as more constitutive. So instead of looking at, say, a film about US forces operating in Iraq (e.g. *The Hurt Locker*) and asking whether it offers a realistic portrayal of the conflict, we ask different kinds of questions. How does the action-thriller reinforce or unsettle particular framings of the US-led invasion and occupation of Iraq? Do these artistic interventions help to constitute public understandings of key actors and places, and are they all the more significant when watched and engaged with by audiences that are not likely to have any experience of the places cited? Finally, do popular cultural manifestations such as film, television, video games, books, and so on remind us that geopolitics is fundamentally performance based? Like the generic categories we associate with film and television, are there different kinds of geopolitics based on action-thrillers, dramas, horrors, disaster, romance, and fantasy? What difference would it have made if President Bush, rather than choosing to re-create a Reagan-era techno-thriller in May 2003, had chosen a rather different generic category and film such as a humanitarian drama or a legal-judicial pursuit of criminals rather than terrorists?

In this chapter, the interconnection between popular culture and geopolitics is emphasized. They are considered inseparable rather than simply as popular culture acting as a window onto the real world of geopolitics. My interest is, as a consequence, not in whether something is either realistic and/or fantastical. Popular mediums such as film and television have, over the decades, been judged to be significant interventions in the making of geopolitical cultures. As we discuss, television series such as *24* and *The Wire* (but you can add others to the list such as *Homeland* and *Battlestar Galatica*) have all been cited as helping to constitute public understandings of the War on Terror, for example. What matters, moreover, is that we also understand those who consume such popular geopolitics as active subjects who are capable of bringing a range of intertextual knowledge and practices to bring to bear on particular media outputs. Media scholars use terms such as intertextuality to highlight how audiences construct meaning and utilize 'common-sense' understandings of geopolitics and security. One area of particular concern is how far it makes sense to impose any distinction between 'reality' and 'fiction' given the high degree of interaction and interpenetration of what James Der Derian terms the military-industrial-media-entertainment complex (MIME-NET). All of which, he suggests, led to the ever greater blurring between the civilian and the military, real and simulation, and producers and consumers.

Popular geopolitics and media cultures

It is perhaps surprising that classical geopolitical writers such as Halford Mackinder have not focused on popular geopolitics earlier rather than formal educational and citizenship structures. For Mackinder, material objects such as atlases and globes were deserving of greater scrutiny. Popular communication and media cultures have been radically transformed in the intervening period from post-1945 mass television ownership to a contemporary era characterized by multi-media environments, smart technologies, and greater capacity of citizens, especially in the West, to customize their engagements with media such as television and video games. Each of us has our own 'media signature', which is shaped by our access, ownership, production, and interaction to various media objects and organizations including newspapers, radio, television, smart phones, video games, and the internet.

The production, circulation, and consumption of news and entertainment is inherently uneven and unequal as some agents and communities are better able to produce, circulate, and access different sources. In terms of formal news production, for example, large corporations such as CNN International, Time-Warner, News International, and the BBC often loom large. They are extremely significant in terms of determining broadcasting content and scheduling, notwithstanding national and international regimes, which can and do exercise some control over audience environments. The newspaper report, the television broadcast, and the internet podcast help determine which people, places, and events are judged to be newsworthy. Such choices then influence viewers' responses, with stories about victims and perpetrators, exploiters and exploited, named individuals and groups and the nameless. Notwithstanding the exponential expansion of so-called citizen journalism and smart phone technologies (including video recording facilities armed with email and twitter-based functionality), media producers such as the BBC are still accorded considerable importance in terms of how their broadcasting material is scrutinized and judged. Media cultures vary greatly from place to place.

Given the capacity of mass media if widely circulated to shape and influence public opinion both domestically and overseas, it is not surprising that governments, both democratic and authoritarian, have sought to regulate, monitor, disrupt, and ban broadcasting. On the eve of a controversial Commonwealth Heads of State meeting in Sri Lanka in November 2013, a British news channel (Channel 4) was instrumental in broadcasting video material appearing to show Sri Lankan forces executing prisoners, including civilians, in the midst of a long-standing and brutal civil war lasting some 25 years. In a series of programmes entitled *Sri Lanka's Killing Fields*, Channel 4 detailed a number of examples where civilians were murdered in the final weeks of the civil war in 2009. The footage of the deaths comes from both survivors of the violence and so-called 'war trophy' coverage caught by government soldiers on their mobile phones. As a consequence of such video material, there is growing pressure for the UN to order a formal investigation into Sri Lankan government forces and alleged crimes against humanity. The British prime minister was widely condemned for attending the summit but committed the UK government, as the ex-colonial power and core funder of the Commonwealth, to pursue the matter further. Channel 4 news journalists complained of Sri Lankan government harassment.

What was noteworthy about the controversy was not only the horrific abuses being discussed in a context where Sri Lanka will be better known to many as a holiday destination (notwithstanding the violent civil war and controversial status of the Tamil Tigers) but the role of smart phone footage taken by civilians and military personal and the way in which that acts to shape and frame geopolitical representations and interventions. Was Sri Lanka in the grip of a civil war? Or was the Colombo-based government fighting against a terror group (Tamil Tigers) and violent separatism? And this is not unique to Sri Lanka in terms of how media coverage shapes geopolitical framing. In November 2013, a member of the British armed forces was jailed for murdering an Afghan combatant after mobile phone coverage of the event itself was discovered by accident on one of the soldier's personal computers. Had this chance discovery not been made, the soldier in question may never have been brought to trial. Some of the video footage, and sound footage, has been made public and gone viral. Social media forums such as Facebook and Twitter have enabled such materials to be discussed more widely. And it clearly challenges, as we noted in Chapter 5, more official efforts on behalf of the UK government to represent British involvement in Afghanistan as peacekeeping and humanitarian in nature.

The geopolitical power of the media, therefore, lies not only in the nature of the broadcasting itself but also the manner in which events, people, and places are 'framed' (Figure 14). The latter is a term used in media studies to describe the way in which a story is explained to viewers or listeners. The circulation of images and news broadcasting can also act as provocation to governments, social movements, and others to demand action. Viewers might have reacted by phoning friends to commiserate, written letters to newspapers, emailed government departments, circulated video imagery, started Facebook campaigns, and composed tweets. In different ways, therefore, the representations of places and people can and do provoke all kinds of emotional investments and

14. FIFA announcement of Qatar as the host of the 2022 World Cup, Zurich, 2 December 2012. It later became clear that the preparation process was being undertaken by migrant workers living in grim circumstances

demands for political action. Activists are able to challenge the dominant framings and representations of geopolitics using the social media platform, Facebook, and video sharing sites such as YouTube. So what matters, therefore, is what does not get broadcast as well as what does.

For many in the Middle East and the Islamic world, events such as the civil war in Syria, the Arab Spring, and Israeli-Iranian tension have been animated and magnified by formal and increasingly social media (Box 17). It is now difficult to imagine not witnessing, via social media, citizen journalism of major events such as the overthrow of governments, the exposure of atrocities such as massacres and chemical weapons attacks, and civil conflict. If anything, these kinds of images and sounds have challenged ideas and understandings of civilian populations who are increasingly willing and able to promote their demands. Moreover, it unsettles dominant geopolitical framings, which for much of the last decade have been seen in the West through the prism of the War on

Box 17. We love you: YouTube, Israel, and Iran

In March 2012, Israeli peace activists posted a short video on YouTube featuring a number of Israeli men, women, and children reassuring Iranians watching the film that they did not 'hate' Iran. Moreover, many of them were shown to be making the point that they actively challenged the claims made by the Israeli government that Iran represented an existential threat to Israel. With John Lennon's 'Imagine' song playing in the background, the footage of ordinary Israelis professing to 'love' Iran even if they admit they have never visited the country or met an Iranian was intended to contest the mainstream geopolitical framing of this neighbour as threatening. While the audience size in Iran is not known, the video itself was part of a wider anti-war movement in Israel contesting the possibility of military strikes against nuclear and military infrastructure within Iran. A Facebook campaign 'Israel Loves Iran' was also launched at the same time.

The Israel Loves Iran is as much a peace movement as it is a social media initiative. But it is also an example of public diplomacy, which is not tied to either the Israeli or Iranian governments. Established by an Israeli graphic designer, Ronny Edry, his initial posting on Facebook declaring that 'Iranians, we love you, we will never bomb your country' encouraged further campaigning and inspired an Iran Loves Israel movement (founded by Majid Nowrouzi). Such initiatives have also encouraged third party meetings and video/photographic exchanging, frequently depicting everyday contexts including family life. Edry and Nowrouzi later met in person in the United States and there has been some campaigning to get the pair nominated for the Nobel Peace Prize.

Terror. As the Syrian civil war demonstrates there are a series of religious, ethnic, and transnational alliances and loyalties involving Iran, Turkey, Qatar, Saudi Arabia, Russia, Hezbollah, Lebanon, and a suite of non-governmental and humanitarian organizations such as International Rescue and the Red Crescent at play. And reporting and commenting on such events and their ramifications (including the external actors involved) remains fraught with personal danger for journalists, both professional and civilian.

Hollywood and cold war 'national security cinema'

For much of the last century, the United States has not experienced the ravages of war and mass disaster in a way that has been routine in some parts of the world. The assault on Pearl Harbor in December 1941 and the September 11th attacks are usually taken to be the two major exceptions to the rule. Despite the shock of both events and the loss of life, these two episodes pale into comparison with the losses experienced in places such as France, Belgium, and the Soviet Union. While many Americans died in Europe during the two world wars, such conflict did not penetrate American shores. American film companies, despite this absence of conflict on American territory, have been particularly significant in upholding the aphorism that war is often fought twice—once on the battlefield and once on film. As one of the characters in *Wag the Dog* (1997) tells his companions, 'war is show business'.

As America's direct experience of war is more limited, Hollywood generated a whole series of films, labelled 'national security cinema', which outlined in a highly imaginative way threats facing the United States. The list is a long one and includes Soviet and other communist forces, Nazis, terrorists, extraterrestrials, meteors, uncontrollable natural forces and machines. Given the widespread popularity of Hollywood productions both inside and outside the United States, it is understandable that films have been viewed as an important contributor to America's visions of its own standing and significance in the world. For many people outside the country, Hollywood films are usually their first point of contact with this country of 300 million inhabitants.

During the cold war, most Americans neither encountered a Soviet citizen nor travelled to the Soviet Union. The same could be said for Communist China and a host of other regimes of which the United States disapproved. The few that did were likely to be members of the armed forces, the business community, artists, sportsmen and women, and of course spies. For most Americans, Churchill's description of an 'iron curtain' across Europe seemed perfectly reasonable, as it did for many Europeans on either side of the Central/Eastern European divide. Film, radio, and later television footage played a crucial role in shaping American impressions of the Soviet Union and the threat posed by communism inside and outside their country. It also helped to consolidate in the main a sense of American self-identity—the land of the free, a beacon of democracy, and a liberal 'way of life' that President Truman had described in 1947.

Film historians have contended that American cold war cinema was at its most important in the 1940s and 1950s. In an era before mass ownership of television, people flocked to the cinema not only to watch films but also to access newsreels and documentaries shown alongside the main feature. What makes these films all the more significant is that Hollywood production companies were closely aligned to various organs of government departments such as the State and Defense Departments in Washington, DC. In 1948, the Pentagon established a special liaison office as part of the Assistant Secretary of Defense for Public Affairs and the latter was extremely important in shaping story lines and determining whether cooperation would be extended to any production wishing to use American military equipment or personnel. Films such as *The Longest Day* (1961) enjoyed Pentagon support even if some of the US military personnel had to be withdrawn from the filmset because of the worsening crisis in Berlin, which culminated with the East Germans building the wall which divided the city until November 1989.

The Pentagon worked closely with producers such as Frank Capra and provided advice, equipment, and personnel for his *Why We Fight* series. The latter was required viewing for all US servicemen and women. This series in particular highlighted the significance attached to visual media by the American authorities in shaping military and public opinion. Given the scale of the threat apparently posed by the Soviet Union, it was not surprising that other agencies such as the US Information Agency and the Central Intelligence Agency (CIA) conceived of film as a vital element in the public campaign to educate American citizens about the dangers posed by the Soviets and to inform others outside the nation as well. The CIA provided secret funding for the animated film, *Animal Farm*, which was released in 1954, precisely because George Orwell's imprint was deemed to be highly appropriate given his allusions to the failed promises of the 1917 Russian Revolution.

During the 1940s and 1950s, Hollywood production companies did not need government funding or interference to persuade them that the Soviet Union and communism more generally posed a danger to the American way of life. America and the Soviet Union had, in this era, clashed over the future of Berlin and the Korean Peninsula. In 1949, the Soviets were confirmed as a nuclear power aided and abetted by the spy Klaus Fuchs. Films such as *My Son John* (1952), *Red Planet Mars* (1952), and *The Thing* (1951) made connections between the threats and dangers facing the American public in this uncertain period. While the first film highlighted the power of communism to influence and undermine the moral compasses of young people, the second and third focused on the dangers posed by aliens to the national security of the country. Taken together, the films seem to suggest that never-ending vigilance was required and that dangerous idealism regarding communism had to be contained.

As with the practical geopolitical reasoning of the Truman administration, films such as *My Son John* (1952) contribute to a particular geographical representation of the United States and its sense of self-identity. The openness and tolerance of the United States are shown to be both a virtue and a threat to its very existence. It is precisely because people, ideas, and goods can move freely throughout its national territory that loyal and patriotic citizens have to be ever vigilant. Given these kinds of conditions, impressionistic young people are portrayed as particularly vulnerable to such porosity and the malign influence of a certain type of intellectual. The Soviet Union, by way of contrast, was depicted as a Red Menace in a manner already outlined in the writings of George Kennan in documents such as NSC-68: geographically expansive, culturally monolithic, religiously suspect, and politically ceaseless in its desire to corrupt the body politic of America. According to some sections of Hollywood, this threat posed by the Soviets was also capable of subcontracting foreigners and possibly even space aliens to continue the struggle for world domination.

American political and religious figures such as William Buckley, Billy Graham, and John Foster Dulles also added to this potent discussion and dissection of the Soviet Union and the Red Menace. Graham in particular emphasized the profound differences between the godless Soviet Union and Christian America. Further cementing the popular significance of extremely conservative films like those described above was the political assault unleashed by the Committee on Un-American Activities of the House of Representatives (HUAC) in the late 1940s and early 1950s. The committee opened its hearings in 1947 and heard submissions from 'friendly witnesses': producers, screenwriters, and actors associated with the motion picture industry. A total of 41 people were interviewed and a number of other people associated with the industry were accused of holding left-wing views.

Thereafter, the committee concentrated its energies on the so-called 'Hollywood 10'—a group of individuals who refused to answer any questions and claimed the First Amendment of the US Constitution as their right to do so. The committee disagreed with their stance and all were jailed for their dissent. With the help of the FBI, the Catholic League of Decency, and the American Legion, a list was produced called the *Red Channels*, which contained information about anyone working in Hollywood judged to have a subversive past. Unlike those who appeared before the committee and convinced its members of their innocence, these individuals were blacklisted and effectively denied employment as writers, actors, or producers. Over 300 people including Charlie Chaplin and Orson Wells were listed as having suspect pasts. The impact on Hollywood was considerable and unsurprisingly did not encourage a visual culture of dissent from the predominantly conservative view of the cold war as a political-religious confrontation between the United States and its enemies.

This of course is not to presume that all producers, film critics, and movie watchers uncritically accepted the geopolitical representations of the Red Menace. Some producers used science fiction and the spectre of aliens to explore radically different interpretations of the cold war zeitgeist. Jack Arnold's *It Came from Outer Space* (1953) featured a group of visiting aliens condemning America's fear of strangers and the unknown. Small-town America is shown to be bigoted and xenophobic in its confrontation with strangers. Stanley Kramer's adaptation of *On the Beach* (1959) depicted the horrors of nuclear annihilation and questioned the strategic logic of nuclear confrontation. Despite government condemnation, the film was one of the highest grossing productions in the year of its release. Another film by Stanley Kramer, *High Noon* (1952), told the tale of a sheriff (Will

Kane, played by Gary Cooper) who is refused help by local people even though a gang determined to extract revenge following their earlier arrest threatens his life. For some within Hollywood, the film was immediately seen as a satire on the activities of HUAC and the members of the motion picture industry who colluded with their blacklisting activities.

Between the late 1940s and 1960, the motion picture industry produced well over 4,000 films, with only a fraction genuinely critical of the conservative American understandings of the cold war and geopolitical representations of the Soviet Union and the communist threat. Hollywood, encouraged by the HUAC hearings and later the investigations conducted by Senator Joseph McCarthy, found it easier to produce films that reproduced rather than undermined those implicit understandings of the United States as a country composed of god-fearing, liberty-loving souls determined to resist being seduced by godless Soviets and their extraterrestrial accomplices.

In retrospect, it is clear that during the most intense phases of the cold war (the 1940s and 1950s) and later during the 1980s, Hollywood was at its most conservative in terms of its visual representations of the cold war. As a teenager, I vividly recall with some incredulity watching the film *Red Dawn* (1984), which opens with a parachute assault by Soviet and Cuban forces on an American school somewhere in the Midwest of America and eventually concludes with a group of schoolchildren successfully leading a counter-assault on these occupying forces. Other productions such as *Top Gun* (1986) seem to fit with a period characterized by renewed cold war tension, American determination to purge communist forces in Latin America and to financially and militarily assist others such as Afghan rebels in their resistance to the Soviet Union. While American service personnel or citizens inevitably prevailed, these kinds of films alongside *Firefox* (1984) and *Rambo Part II* (1986) either celebrated American technological prowess (and associated way of life) or depicted hyper-masculine individuals able to overcome extreme odds. Fact and fiction frequently blurred as President Reagan made references to the filmic exploits of Rambo while explaining to the American people particular security threats facing the country.

The locations depicted in these late cold war films are significant as they often highlight the apparent danger posed by regimes found in Central America, South-East Asia, and the Middle East. One trend that was to become more apparent following the 1991 Gulf War was the emergence of films that depicted Islamic terrorists operating from places such as Beirut. This coincidence was not accidental as American forces had been disastrously deployed in the Lebanon in 1983. In October of that year, a truck bomb killed over 200 US Marines in their Beirut-based barracks. Shortly afterwards films appeared such as *Iron Eagle* (1985) and *Navy Seals* (1985), which took as their geographical backdrop either the Lebanon or the wider Middle East. Importantly, these places and their inhabitants were depicted as irrational, demonic, and prone to violence, especially against American and Western personnel and interests. In the case of *Top Gun*, which enjoyed substantial cooperation from the US Navy, the producers were told that the combat action had to be filmed over an ocean. During the film, the airborne location is described as somewhere over the Indian Ocean and the enemy pilots are shown to have red stars embossed on their flight helmets but their identity is never confirmed. As the ocean closest to the Middle East, the possibility of those planes being from regional proxies of the Soviet Union is not implausible.

For Arab-American groups, these types of popular geopolitical representations were disturbing, precisely because they felt that their own community was in danger of being aligned en masse with terrorism and anti-American activities. This fear was, of course, to be amplified after the American assault on Iraqi forces in Kuwait from January 1991 onwards. By that stage, it was apparent that the Soviet Union no longer posed a serious military threat to the United States, as the cold war confrontation was widely considered over, following the demolition of the Berlin Wall in November 1989. This did not imply, however, that it would not pose a threat to the United States ever again. When Hollywood did depict the post-cold war former Soviet Union in films such as *Goldeneye* (1995), *Air Force One* (1997), and the *Peacemaker* (1997), it was invariably represented as chaotic, fragmented, and a source of terrorism or arms trafficking. Alternatively, a production such as *Hunt for Red October* (1990), while raising the spectre of a possible naval assault on the United States, ultimately depicts a Soviet submarine captain and his fellow officers anxious to escape to the United States and enjoy the fruits of the American dream.

Before the 11 September attacks, post-cold war films concerning acts of terror in the United States were largely suggestive rather than grounded in substantial human experience. While there was an attack on the World Trade Center in 1993 and an attack on a federal building in Oklahoma City in 1996, Hollywood did not respond in the same way as it did following 9/11 (Box 18). Films such as *Speed* (1994) and *The Rock* (1996) depicted acts of terror carried out by disgruntled American police and military officers angry with the federal government or specific institutions such as the Los Angeles Police Department. Whereas the destruction of New York had been imagined cinematically in productions such as *Planet of the Apes* (1968), the deadly assault by 19 hijackers produced much existential discussion about the future of the United States, and Hollywood was quickly mobilized by the George W. Bush administration as one element in the response to this event and the subsequent self-declared War on Terror.

Box 18. Flying the flag: Hollywood, 9/11, and the War on Terror

In the aftermath of the 11 September 2001 attacks, the US media reported a meeting between representatives from the George W. Bush administration and the movie and entertainment industry. Spearheaded by presidential adviser Karl Rove and Jack Valenti, the chair of the Motion Picture Association of America, the idea of the meeting in November 2001 was to explore ways in which popular culture might play a role in promoting homeland security and explaining the declaration of a War on Terror. While denying that the administration was asking the entertainment industry to produce movies and television shows 'glorifying' the president, there was interest in exploring how popular media might be used to be 'informative' and 'supportive'.

Between 2001 and 2009 (i.e. President Bush's terms of office), as a consequence, there was considerable interest in exploring how popular culture contributed to the construction and diffusion of the War on Terror. Cartoons, television shows, films, novels, music, and other outputs including objects such as number plates and souvenirs were investigated. For the critics, they detected a tendency within mainstream media and entertainment productions to reproduce through objects and images a framing that supported the US troops in Afghanistan and Iraq, that ensured that the federal government should not be blamed in any way for the 9/11 attacks, and for endorsing the view that the United States was engaged in a global fight against terrorists and terrorism. In short, it is argued that such outputs contributed and sustained an aggressive form of US nationalism and geopolitics, lionizing the role of the United States and its fighting forces in particular.

Television and War on Terror: the case of serial shows

Television has arguably been the most important popular medium for transmitting about and engaging with the War on Terror. While there have been a slew of films addressing the War on Terror, originating out of Hollywood and other cinematic cultures, US-based television shows such *24*, *The Wire*, *Homeland*, and *Battlestar Galactica* have earned popular and critical acclaim for their engagement with terrorism, war, homeland security, and torture. They have also been hugely controversial as well. The award-winning series *24* is an excellent example. Over eight seasons (running between 2001 and 2010), the real-time serial drama follows the exploits of counter-terror officer Jack Bauer and his efforts to ensure the security of high-profile individuals, family members, and entire cities within the United States. The show premiered in November 2001 and enjoyed audience figures running into the millions. Each episode covered one hour only and the show's signature ticking clock was intended to remind audiences of the real-time pressures facing counter-terror officers.

One area of considerable controversy throughout the series was Bauer's use of extraordinary methods such as torture and extreme forms of interrogation. Bauer's modus operandi stimulated a great deal of public discussion at the time and led to fears that this was endorsing the use of extraordinary (and indeed extra-judicial) force in the face of anxieties about terrorism and fears of possible repeats of attacks of the scale and size of the 11 September assault. For critics, the producers of *24* were complicit with US government discourses and practices, calling for extraordinary measures to ensure that the United States did not endure a 'second 9/11'. What became apparent following 9/11 was that military and intelligence officials were engaging in similar techniques shown to be the provenance of Jack Bauer. What made the show even more controversial was growing evidence that the FBI and CIA were actively involved in advising and assisting the entertainment industry in its depictions of the War on Terror. Chase Brandon, the CIA's representative in Hollywood, was said to be an adviser for the *24* scripts.

But there is another element of *24* that is of relevance to popular geopolitics, namely a focus on what kind of people and places get depicted as threatening or dangerous and by association those that are deemed worthy of protecting and saving. *24*, with its action-thriller qualities, made it an ideal vehicle to project dramatic narratives involving 'Turkish' terrorists and others including Lebanese, Russian, and Serbian, and other groups who appear to be determined to unleash terrorist violence against nuclear reactors, shopping malls, work places, highways, airports, and suburban neighbourhoods in Los Angeles. What one might take away from Bauer's multifarious exploits is that the sites and spaces of terror are literally everywhere and there are few areas of public life that might not be vulnerable to a terrorist attack: a point made by senior members of the Bush administration who, on introducing the homeland security terror alert system, warned US Citizens that they needed to be vigilant everywhere. As President Bush warned the American people in January 2002, 'A terrorist underworld— including groups like Hamas, Hezbollah, Islamic Jihad, Jaish-i-Mohammed—operates in remote jungles and deserts, and hides in the centers of large cities… But some governments will be timid in the face of terror. And make no mistake about it: if they do not act, America will.'

While *24* has been regarded as a neo-conservative endorsement of the need for widespread and ruthless counter-terrorism, it has also informed public critique of the War on Terror (Box 19). Other television shows such as *The Wire* (2002–8), based on the experiences of police officers, criminals, city officials, and others in a poverty-ridden and financially insecure Baltimore, is credited with offering a different view of how the war on drugs, the War on Terror, and policing inform one another. The very title 'The Wire' indicates a central conceit of the show, which was to focus on

Box 19. States of exception and exceptional states

The state of exception has attracted much attention and writers such as Carl Schmitt in the 1920s and 1930s explored the relationship between law, politics, sovereignty, and emergencies. Schmitt's interest in the exceptional was predicated on a belief that what made the sovereign powerful was not the regulation of the 'normal' but the implementation of the 'exceptional'. By declaring a state of emergency or imposing martial law, for example, the sovereign ruler or government shows its hand in terms of defining what is permissible and what is not. Films such as *The Siege* (1998) and *Enemy of the State* (1988) offered a glimpse, in a pre-9/11 setting, of how the 'emergency' can be used to claim a necessity for exceptional powers without the normal constraints of law and policing.

More recent authors such as Giorgio Agamben have questioned whether the 'state of exception' is actually that exceptional. In other words, is there evidence to suggest that states are often by default exceptional in their nature, as modern governments claim, and incorporate the powers to defer the rule of law in order to address challenges, particularly those labelled as security challenges? As a consequence, the boundary between law and the exception becomes increasingly blurred as the state normalizes the state of exception itself. Critics of the War on Terror argue that practices such as extraordinary rendition, drone attacks, targeted assassinations, mass surveillance, and the like reveal this very exceptionality and increasingly the use of either new laws and/or covert action to circumvent and, increasingly, justify these exceptional practices. Moreover, citizens themselves are also asked to help perpetuate these appeals to exceptionality by spying on one another and reporting wherever possible 'suspicious behaviour'.

objects essential to the business of electronic surveillance. Frustrated by their inability to prosecute a major drug-dealing family, the Baltimore police turn to surveillance and exceptional measures, including violence, to disrupt the city's drugs economy. While drugs remain the primary object of concern rather than terror (as in the case of *24*), the series considers how urban America is nonetheless caught in a broader matrix of geopolitical matters including neo-liberal restructuring and security politics.

While located in Baltimore, the political, economic, and cultural challenges facing this multi-racial city are not exclusive to North-East America but also linked to the fate of other places in the world. Global flows of drug smuggling (the international criminal that supplies the Barksdale family is known as 'The Greek') and corporate/financial investment have left their mark on the physical infrastructure of the city and the residents in multiple sites including public education, media, and local government. *The Wire* suggests that the war on drugs, like the War on Terror, is not just an abstract slogan but also indicative of a set of relationships that tie people and places together. In Season 5, in particular, the show explores how the police and law enforcement agencies carry out the war on drugs, resisted by local residents and framed by media coverage. It is particularly insightful on the impact of particular police-led strategies regarding the drugs trade, insisting that raids and surveillance regimes end up alienating local communities and making it less likely that residents will support attempts to regulate or even eradicate the drugs trade. Some residents are more affected by these anti-drug strategies than others, and in particular the poor and African-American communities are depicted as being on the sharp end of the war on drugs. For those charged with waging such anti-drug campaigns, the effects are shown to be counter-productive, corrupting, destructive, and disillusioning.

If you see anything
suspicious, report it
to our staff or
the police immediately.

MAYOR
OF LONDON   POLICE   Transport
for London

15. A daily reminder of the need for vigilance: 'see anything suspicious' poster, Transport for London

Unlike *24*, *The Wire* is arguably a powerful critique of the state of exception. It is a cautionary tale of what can happen when the state declares war on an object or an activity. It turns the geopolitical gaze not to external others but to the local, the everyday, and the mundane but powerful consequences of surveillance, raiding, and violence. The primary sites of geopolitics are the streets, the schools, the docks, and the police stations (Figure 15). It asks us to consider the legitimacy and efficacy of violence and whether state-sanctioned violence is any less exceptional and disturbing than the violence of the gangs and criminals. The police and the drug families are shown to be similar—hierarchical, rule-based, irrational, and capable of unpredictable behaviour. Both are inhabited by a plethora of 'petty sovereigns' who, in Judith Butler's terms, are men (overwhelmingly) capable of acting in extraordinary ways, which are barely accountable and regulated at times. When posed as a security risk, drugs and terror share commonalities including a penchant for 'working the dark side', 'taking the gloves off', and operating in 'the shadows'.

The internet and a popular geopolitics of dissent

Since the 1980s, the growth and development of the internet has been widely championed as encouraging further social interaction and shrinking geographical distance. The United States remains by far the biggest user community of the internet and the most significant producer of information. The digital divide between North America, Europe, and East Asia, on the one hand, and sub-Saharan Africa and the Middle East, on the other, remains stark, even though internet access is becoming more widespread in both the latter regions. Powerful search engines such as Google allow users to access and download images and stories in mere seconds with both positive and negative consequences, ranging from the fear of seditious and offensive material being published on the internet to people being able to access new communities and social networks in a virtual manner. This has clearly allowed all kinds of activities to flourish, including global terror networks and neo-Nazi groupings. Al-Qaeda has used the internet to generate funding, send encoded messages to members, publicize videos of speeches by its leaders, and to promote activities across the world. Much to the frustration of national governments, the internet is extremely difficult to police and patrol as websites can be shut down but then re-emerge shortly afterwards with a different domain address.

The internet has provided an important medium for the anti-globalization movement and enabled it to challenge both the material power of states, corporations, and institutions associated with the dominant political-economic order and to contest particular visual and textual representations of that dominant architecture. In the case of the first dimension, the anti-globalization movement has publicized and organized global days of action, usually in cities which happen to be hosting meetings of the WTO, IMF, or the G8. More widely, the internet has facilitated the growth and development of social networks such as the People's Global Action and the World Social Forum, both of which have enabled activists all over the world to come together to consider alternatives to neo-liberalism and solutions to local issues such as water privatization in South Africa, land ownership in Mexico, and the impact of foreign debt repayments in Latin America.

The internet has therefore allowed individuals and groups committed to protesting about neo-liberal forms of globalization to exchange experiences, plan action, swap dates, and highlight future events in a way that is clearly far quicker than in the past. The demonstrations organized during a World Trade Organization (WTO) meeting in Seattle during November and December 1999 coincided with what has been called e-mobilization and e-protest. Moreover, the capacity to circulate images alongside commentaries has also been important in allowing these groups to promote their particular viewpoints and potentially to shape the news agendas, even though many campaigners complain that mainstream media tends to marginalize their protests and demands for radical reforms of the neo-liberal world economy and its servicing institutions such as the WTO or powerful groupings such as the G8.

Contesting dominant representations of the prevailing global politico-economic order is another area of activity facilitated by the internet and other media. Corporate television broadcasts of G8 and WTO summits tend, in the opinion of anti-globalization movements, to reinforce rather than challenge the geopolitics of neo-liberalism. Attention is usually granted to heads of states and their delegations as opposed to protestors who tend to be viewed as a distraction or, increasingly in the aftermath of 9/11, as a security challenge which needs to be contained. As the ownership of the media becomes increasingly concentrated in the hands of larger corporations such as News International, this tendency is likely to increase rather than diminish. As with powerful economies such as the United States and Japan, there is a tendency to support the politico-economic status quo and that includes its accompanying political architecture, which helps to regulate the interaction between territories and flows of people, investment, and trade.

Websites and alternative media sources (e.g. www.indymedia.org.uk) have been used routinely to convey a rather different vision of the world—an unequal one where the richest 20 per cent of the world possess 90 per cent of global income. These sites have also encouraged campaigners to submit news stories and images of global days of action and to submit items about local places and their geographical connections to global processes such as trade, investment, and foreign debt. The Zapatista movement in Mexico and its leadership have pioneered much of this investment in the internet and alternative media, recognizing in the early 1990s that the media were a crucial component in their struggles to resist the Mexican state, international financial markets, and the prevailing global economic order. What made their usage so surprising was that internet connectivity was low in Southern Mexico. Within two years of launching their counter-offensive against neo-liberalism, the Zapatistas had organized a series of continental and intercontinental meetings in 1996 and 1997 through the use of the internet and email. Thousands attended the meetings and exchanged information with one another, including the American film producer Oliver Stone. The charismatic leader of the Zapatistas (Marcos) used the internet to publicize their causes (land dispossession, economic marginalization, and racial discrimination) and encouraged new networks of solidarity in Mexico, Latin America, and beyond. The internet provides a forum for the group to continue their struggle and is also successful in encouraging other groups and individuals to formulate alternative understandings of the global economy, international financial markets, and the Mexican economy. So in that sense the internet was seen, in some quarters, as enabling new networks of geopolitical solidarity.

As other governments have discovered, however, controlling information posted on the internet can be controversial and difficult, given the efforts of hackers to undermine government established firewalls and some hacking organizations have explicitly targeted government agencies and corporate web-based accounts in order to expose information security flaws or register such acts as a form of dissent. In the aftermath of 9/11, the US Congress passed the Patriot Act and other legislation such as the 2007 Protect America Act, which enables the Executive and key agencies such as the National Security Agency to investigate internet and email traffic of those suspected of engaging in activities likely to be harmful to the United States. Other states such as Britain have also sought to impose greater surveillance and control over information users considered suspect. The monitoring of individuals and groups, in the name of counter-terrorism, has been extremely significant in terms of governments trying to restore the prevailing geopolitical architecture of sovereign states, borders, surveillance, and national territories. Since the revelations of Edward Snowden in May 2013, an employee of the National Security Agency (NSA), public knowledge of mass surveillance (often warrantless spying), and specifically data-mining programs such as PRISM have heightened debate about the manner in which internet access and usage is routinely monitored by intelligence agencies including the NSA and CIA. Snowden not only released scores of documents but also revealed how mass surveillance involved international cooperation with other intelligence agencies around the world, telecommunication companies, and internet providers such as Google. When former Vice President Dick Chenney called for 'total information awareness', it was perhaps not apparent at the time how this quest would lead to what some have described as a surveillance-internet-industrial complex. When still a presidential candidate, Senator Obama was critical of the national security state and mass surveillance, but his critical stance softened on assuming presidential office. It is unlikely, for example, that President Obama will grant individuals such as Snowden any kind of immunity from prosecution.

Conclusions

This chapter has shown how popular geopolitics can be studied with reference to the media and clearly could be extended to consider in greater detail radio, cartoons and/or music. While established media forms such as newspapers, television, and radio remain highly significant in producing and circulating news about the world, it is new media forms such as the internet and associated practices such as blogging and podcasting that will command increasing attention from those interested in popular geopolitics. As interconnectivity increases, especially in the Middle East, the internet is providing not only an opportunity for viewers to access different news sources but also to articulate their opinions online. In countries and regions where the public sphere is tightly controlled by national governments, bloggers are an increasingly significant presence even if their activities have been subject to harassment, imprisonment, and ongoing surveillance. Iranian bloggers provide fascinating insights into contemporary Iran and offer dissenting opinions with regards to Iran's foreign policy choices, which help explain to interested readers why, for example, many online commentators feel threatened by the military powers of the United States, Israel, Pakistan, India, and China. Unlike Iran, all these states possess substantial stocks of weapons of mass destruction.

We should not, for one moment, assume that new media practices such as blogging are not important in other places too. In the

United States, liberal academics and commentators have frequently bemoaned the fact that so much of American mainstream media is corporately owned and politically conservative. With ever-growing revelations relating to mass surveillance and data mining, there may well be further popular geopolitical resistance to such intrusions into the lives of citizens. For comedians such as Jon Stewart and Stephen Colbert the Snowden revelations have provided rich comedic material in challenging the presumption that US administrations should enjoy such exceptional powers and they have enjoyed speculating on which countries might be able to offer the fugitive analyst some kind of asylum. The point of all of this is to remind us that geopolitics, for all its seriousness, is also capable of generating jokes and satirical comedy but is also brought to bear through such mediums as well as television, film, novels, cartoons, and so on.

References

Chapter 1: It's essential to be geopolitical!

President George W. Bush State of the Union Address, 29 January 2002 <http://www.npr.org/news/specials/sou/2002/020129. bushunion.html>.

Jeremy Scahill, *Dirty Wars. The World is a Battlefield* (Nation Books, 2013).

Edward Said, *Orientalism* (Penguin, 1978).

Chapter 2: An intellectual poison?

Isaiah Bowman, 'Geography v. geopolitics', *Geographical Review*, 32 (1942), 646–58.

Richard O'Brien, *End of Geography* (Routledge, 1992).

Gearóid Ó Tuathail, *The Geopolitics Reader* (Routledge, 2006), 1.

Frederick Sondern, 'The Thousand Scientists behind Hitler', *Readers Digest*, 6 (1941), 23–7.

Edmund Walsh, *Total Power* (Doubleday, 1948), 21.

H. Kissinger, *The White House Years* (Little, Brown, 1979), 598, and his comments about Chile are available at: <http://en.wikipedia. org/wiki/Chilean_coup_of_1973>.

George Chesney, *The Battle of Dorking* (Lippincott, Grambo & Co, 1871).

Erslune Childer, *Riddle of the Sands* (Smith, Elders & Co, 1903).

Admiral Thomas Mahan, *The Influence of Sea Power upon History 1660–1783* (Little, Brown & Co, 1898).

Fredrick Ratzel, *The Sea as a Source of the Greatness of a People* (R. Oldenbourg, 1901).

Saul Cohen, *Geography and Politics in a Divided World* (Oxford University Press, 1963).

Chapter 3: Geopolitical architectures

J. Nye, 'The Decline of America's "Soft Power"', *Foreign Affairs*, 83 (2004), 20.
Minuteman Project http://www.minutemanproject.com

Chapter 4: Geopolitics and identity

W. Connelly, *Identity/Difference* (University of Minnesota Press, 2002), 64.
J. Agnew, *Making Political Geography* (Arnold, 2002), 143.

Chapter 5: Geopolitics and objects

Trevor Paglen, *An Atlas of Radical Cartography* (Journal of Aesthetics and Protest Press, 2007).

Further reading

Much of the information relating to geopolitical matters available on the web is subject to great change and variation in quality. There are clearly UK and US publications, both print and online, that address matters of geopolitical interest such as *The Economist, The Onion, The Spectator, New Statesman, The National Interest, The Atlantic, Prospect, Dissent, Foreign Policy*, and so on. Many of these magazines also support active blogs as well. Academic journals such as *Geopolitics* and *Political Geography* regularly publish geopolitical analyses. For French-speaking readers, the journal *Herodote* is an excellent starting point and for Italian-speaking readers, the Italian journal of geopolitics, *Limes*, would be of interest.

More generally, search engines such as Google (<www.google.com>) provide ample opportunities to explore the term geopolitics further, mindful of the fact that there are rich engagements of geopolitics outside the Anglophone world.

Chapter 1: It's essential to be geopolitical!

J. Agnew, *Geopolitics* (Routledge, 2003).
D. Armitage, *Foundations of Modern International Thought* (Cambridge University Press, 2013).
K. Dodds, M. Kuus, and J. Sharp (eds.), *The Ashgate Research Companion to Critical Geopolitics* (Ashgate, 2013).
C. Flint, *Introduction to Geopolitics* (Routledge, 2011).
G. Ó Tuathail, *Critical Geopolitics* (Routledge, 1996).

G. Ó Tuathail, S. Dalby, and P. Routledge (eds.), *The Geopolitics Reader* (Routledge, 2006).

Chapter 2: An intellectual poison?

B. Blouet, *Halford Mackinder* (University of Texas Press, 1987).

I. Bowman, *The New World* (World Company, 1921).

K. Dodds and D. Atkinson (eds.), *Geopolitical Traditions* (Routledge, 2000).

T. Garton Ash, *Free World* (Random House, 2004).

D. Haraway, *Primate Visions* (Routledge, 1989).

G. Kearns, *Geopolitics and Empire: The Legacy of Halford Mackinder* (Oxford University Press, 1998).

S. L. O'Hara and M. Heffernan, 'From Geo-strategy to Geo-economics: The "Heartland" and British Imperialism before and after Mackinder', *Geopolitics*, 11/1 (2006), 54–73.

G. Parker, *Geopolitics: Past, Present and Future* (Pinter, 1998).

W. Parker, *Mackinder: Geography as an Aid to Statecraft* (Oxford University Press, 1982).

Chapter 3: Geopolitical architectures

J. Agnew, *Hegemony: The New Shape of Global Power* (Temple University Press, 2005).

J. Agnew and S. Corbridge, *Mastering Space* (Routledge, 1995).

P. Dicken, *Global Shift* (Sage, 2010).

G. Gong, *The 'Standard of Civilization' in International Society* (Oxford University Press, 1984).

M. Hardt and A. Negri, *Empire* (Harvard University Press, 2001).

D. Harvey, *The New Imperialism* (Oxford University Press, 2005).

S. Krasner, *Sovereignty: Organised Hypocrisy* (Princeton University Press, 1999).

P. Mirowski, *Never Let a Serious Crisis Go to Waste: How Neo-Liberalism Survived the Financial Meltdown* (Verso, 2013).

S. Nye, *Soft Power* (Public Affairs, 2004).

N. Smith, *American Empire* (University of California Press, 2003).

M. Steger, *Globalization: A Very Short Introduction* (Oxford University Press, 2003).

R. Wilkinson and K. Pickett, *The Spirit Level: Why Equality is Better for Everyone* (Penguin, 2010).

Chapter 4: Geopolitics and identity

M. Billig, *Banal Nationalism* (Sage, 1995).

G. Dijkink, *National Identity and Geopolitical Visions* (Routledge, 1996).

D. Gregory, *The Colonial Present* (Blackwell, 2004).

S. Huntington, 'The Clash of Civilisations', *Foreign Affairs*, 72 (1993), 22–49.

B. Lewis, *The Crisis of Islam* (Phoenix, 2004).

G. Matthews and S. Goodman (eds.), *Violence and the Limits of Representation* (Palgrave Macmillan, 2013).

D. Moisi, *The Geopolitics of Emotion* (Bodley Head, 2009).

E. Said, 'The Clash of Ignorance', *The Nation* (22 October 2001), available at: <http://www.thenation.com>.

A. Smith, *Chosen Peoples* (Oxford University Press, 2003).

Chapter 5: Geopolitics and objects

A. Barry, *Material Politics: Disputes along the Pipeline* (Wiley-Blackwell, 2013).

J. Bennett, *Vibrant Matter: A Political Ecology of Things* (Duke University Press, 2010).

D. Gregory and A. Pred (eds.), *Violent Geographies* (Routledge, 2006).

D. Miller, *Stuff* (Polity, 2009).

M. Monmonier, *How to Lie with Maps* (University of Chicago Press, 1996).

S. Turkle (ed.), *Evocative Objects: Things We Think With* (MIT Press, 2011).

Chapter 6: Popular geopolitics

G. Agamben, *State of Exception* (Chicago University Press, 2005).

S. Carter and K. Dodds, *International Politics and Film* (Columbia University Press, 2014).

F. Debrix, *Tabloid Terror: War, Culture and Geopolitics* (Routledge, 2007).

D. Holloway, *9/11 and the War on Terror* (Edinburgh University Press, 2008).

M. Power and A. Crampton (eds.), *Cinema and Popular Geopolitics* (Routledge, 2006).

J. Sharp, *Condensing the Cold War* (University of Minnesota Press, 2000).

J.-M. Valantin, *Hollywood, the Pentagon and Washington* (Anthem Press, 2005).

C. Weber, *I am an American: Filming the Fear of Difference* (Intellect, 2012).

Index

Index

SOCIAL MEDIA
Very Short Introduction

Join our community

www.oup.com/vsi

- Join us online at the official Very Short Introductions **Facebook** page.
- Access the thoughts and musings of our authors with our online **blog**.
- Sign up for our monthly **e-newsletter** to receive information on all new titles publishing that month.
- Browse the full range of Very Short Introductions online.
- Read **extracts** from the Introductions for free.
- Visit our library of **Reading Guides**. These guides, written by our expert authors will help you to question again, why you think what you think.
- If you are a teacher or lecturer you can order inspection copies quickly and simply via our website.